FEMINISM AND POLITICAL THEORY

L

Plea

FEMINISM AND POLITICAL THEORY

Judith Evans
Jill Hills
Karen Hunt
Elizabeth Meehan
Tessa ten Tusscher
Ursula Vogel
Georgina Waylen

SAGE Publications
London ● Beverly Hills ● New Delhi

SAGE Publications Ltd
28 Banner Street
London EC1Y 8QE

SAGE Publications Inc
275 South Beverly Drive
Beverly Hills, California 90212

SAGE Publications India Pvt Ltd
C-236 Defence Colony
New Delhi 110 024

British Library Cataloguing in Publication Data

Feminism and political theory.
  1. Feminism   2. Political science
  I. Evans, Judith
  305.4′2   HQ 1154

Library of Congress Catalogue Card Number 85-063639

ISBN 0-8039-9705-1
ISBN 0-8039-9706-X Pbk

Phototypeset by Sunrise Setting, Torquay, Devon
Printed in Great Britain by J.W. Arrowsmith Ltd., Bristol

Contents

Introduction

Jill Hills

This book arose originally from a group of papers presented at the 1985 Annual Conference of the Political Studies Association in Manchester.[1] It can be read in two ways. It is both a collection of readings from political scientists using the traditional tools of political analysis to tackle traditional questions of equality, freedom and justice, and a collection of work by feminists attempting to answer, each in her own way, how far those traditional tools and theoretical constructs can contribute to a feminist political theory.

The book has been written in opposition to those who would argue that traditional political theory cannot be feminist and that feminist theory cannot be political theory: a current divorce which serves the self-interest of the male-dominated political science profession. The failure of the British political science profession to consider feminism as a legitimate subject of study is a recurring theme throughout the book. Very often where women have been recognized within teaching syllabuses it has been in courses targeted specifically at women, as though women's concerns were not a proper subject of study for men. In contrast, women students have been expected to accept both that their gender-specific interests are marginal to the mainstream of political theory and political science, and that the major discourse takes place in male-centred language about male-centred concerns.

The contributors to this book suggest reasons why this split has occurred. Those reasons range from the division between the traditional literature of political theory and that of feminist writers, to the distinction between 'public' and 'private' realms within liberal political theory, and to strategic questions of women's careers within a male profession. But the contributors would differ on whether separate women's studies courses are a 'good' or 'bad' thing. Some would argue, as does Judith Evans, that feminist theory should be integrated into mainstream political theory courses. Others would argue that separate courses are both necessary for women to recognize and articulate their own concerns, separate from men, and also necessary as a conduit for women into the political science profession. Yet others would agree with Elizabeth Meehan that both are needed.

Just as the contributors are divided on the question of the correct venue for the teaching of feminist political theory, so they are also divided on the utility of the tools and constructs of traditional political theory in forming that feminist theory. The book therefore presents no one unified normative, methodological or theoretical perspective. Rather, it makes plain that radical feminism's concern with the organizing construct of patriarchy, and its widening of the construct of the 'public' realm to include the family, challenge both liberal and Marxist political theories.

The book cannot supply one answer to the question, 'What is feminist political theory?'. Instead, it represents the ongoing debate within the feminist movement between those who would see themselves as 'radical', 'socialist' or 'liberal' feminists. For that reason, each of the chapters is prefaced by a personal introduction by the author in which she sets out why she wrote it and where she sees it fitting into that debate. Whatever their intellectual and pedagogical differences, the contributors all believe that feminism in practice cannot advance without feminist theory and that the debate within this book, and the book itself, are part of both the theory and practice of feminism.

The book is presented in four sections. In the first section, Judith Evans considers the problems for feminists using the traditional methodologies of political theory. In the light of her conclusion that such methodologies are value-free, she examines how far some of the feminist theorists have advanced our perception of what a feminist political theory should contain and how we can proceed from this point onwards. She concludes that political theorists should pay far more attention to feminist writings; that although it may not conform, in style, to the tenets of political philosophy, feminist literature brings new life and new vision to social and political theory.

In the second section, where the authors use a historical perspective to examine the development of feminist ideas, Ursula Vogel's chapter focuses on the liberal eighteenth-century debate on women's emancipation. She shows that in the eighteenth century the case for women's emancipation could be made on two different, and in many ways incompatible, grounds. It could be made, on the one hand, on the basis of a universalistic, genderless human nature and, on the other, on the basis of a distinctly feminine character. The one set of arguments was used by the rationalists, the other by the romantics with their ideal of self-femininity. She argues that although these early feminist writers did not bring about the conceptual revolution necessary for the development of feminist political theory, their ideas, taken in their historical context, were genuinely emancipatory in that they contained utopian elements which associated women's liberation with fundamental changes in human relationships and in the nature of political society. Her discussion of this eighteenth-century debate leads her to question whether the very concepts of 'liberty', 'right', 'justice' and 'citizenship' do not contain an in-built bias against the full inclusion of women.

Karen Hunt's chapter looks at a similar debate which took place within the Social Democratic Federation (SDF), Britain's first Marxist party, in the late nineteenth and early twentieth centuries on what came to be called the Woman Question. Her chapter examines how socialists believe women become socialists and how this affects women's perceptions of socialism, asking whether the socialist model of politicization is gender-specific. It highlights the way in which the SDF perceived women both theoretically and practically, arguing in particular that the ambiguities in the socialist construction of the theory of the Woman Question allowed socialist organizations to maintain highly ambivalent positions towards women including outright misogyny. These views did not just reflect an individual's or even a party's idiosyncracies, but were inherent in the ambiguities of the theory. The material has clear ramifications for contemporary discussions on the relationship between socialism and feminism.

The third section of the book is devoted to feminist perspectives on the 'New Right'. Tessa ten Tusscher's chapter looks at the New Right and Thatcherism from a left perspective. She argues that the left's analysis of the New Right's ideology and actions, particularly as they occur in Britain, has been dominated by male-defined analysis; an analysis which, in its emphasis on the economic, fails to explain the moral, traditional and familial aspects of that ideology. She offers an account of the New Right which puts women in the centre of the debate, arguing that its ideas and practical impact can only be fully understood if a gender dimension is added to the left's traditional Marxist analysis. She discusses the crisis in patriarchal relations within recent years and concludes that the explanation for the rise of the New Right has to take place within the context of crises in social democracy and the economy combined with this crisis in patriarchy.

From another perspective, Georgina Waylen's chapter examines the New Right theorization of Hayek and Friedman. She argues that neo-liberal ideas are based on assumptions which subsume women into the family and the private sphere. In theories which raise the concept of a free market to that of a social ethic, any relations outside the market have to be conflated into it, those outside being represented by the head of household, who can then be assumed to be the economic agent. Neo-liberal theories therefore rely on a conflation of the family and the individual with the implication that the private family, and women within it, should take the burden of caring for the old, the young and the sick. Hence she concludes that whereas neo-liberalism talks of liberty for all individuals, in reality it advocates liberty only for men. Further, it would not be possible to put women back into the model, because a consideration of women as individuals would entail a radical restructuring of the family and the protected domain of the 'private' which in turn would entail the destruction of the foundations of neo-liberalism.

The final section of the book is devoted to the relationship between feminism and the study and teaching of politics. Judith Evans's concern that feminists have no adequate conception of politics leads her to examine the contributions of 'liberal', 'radical', and 'Marxist' feminist writers to political theory. She argues that although certain forms of liberal feminism imply the rejection of the public/private split traditionally upheld by political scientists, liberalism, without radical change, has little to offer the feminist cause in that its values of autonomy, tolerance and the preservation of the private realm lead to a contradiction which becomes for feminism an impasse. The major contributions of both radical and Marxist feminism have been also in their attacks on the distinction between the public and private realms. In the concluding paragraphs of her chapter she considers why it is that so few of the writers whom she cites are political scientists, concluding that because of the low proportion of women political scientists the study of women has been downgraded. In turn, this downgrading of women as subjects of study within the discipline has inhibited the development of liberatory feminist thought.

Elizabeth Meehan's chapter also discusses the problem of political science's slowness in dealing with questions about women's rights and role. Her chapter falls into three sections. In the first two sections, she draws on concepts from the sociology of language, to argue that language not only describes but also limits understanding of the world. Apparently simple forms of naming, what has been allowed to count as valid historical knowledge and questions of disciplinary organization have all combined to exclude feminist analysis. This exclusion has been to the detriment not only of women but also of political analysis itself, especially in its exploration of informal processes that lead to inequality in the 'public' sphere. In the third section she argues that the teaching of feminism must take place on two fronts – both separately and in conventional courses – on the grounds that both reform within the discipline and some separation from it are required. In conclusion, she discusses the relationship between how we theorize about society and the nature of our political system, arguing that neither a theoretical nor a practical reconstruction of the 'public' sphere can take place satisfactorily without feminist theory.

Each of the contributors in this book takes a different perspective in applying feminist concepts to traditional political theory and analysis. Each challenges the ability of male-stream theory and analysis to explain adequately the historical and current subordination of women. An evident theme in the book is the present ossification of the study of politics into standard patterns of thought and denomination appropriate to a previous time. Its underlying argument is that feminism is as much the theoretical product of today's society as yesterday's theoreticians were products of theirs; that feminist constructs provide a passage to a more innovatory, eclectic discipline; that feminist theory is political theory and political analysis must include feminist analysis.

We hope that this book will be read by both men and women interested in the study of politics. Political science may not yet have produced its great feminist philosopher, but, in the meantime, in the belief that both feminism in practice and political theory itself will be advanced by feminist debate, we offer this book as a step towards a feminist political theory.

Note
1. Judith Evans wrote the first chapter especially and Jill Hills acted as co-ordinator for the book.

I

AN OVERVIEW OF THE PROBLEM FOR FEMINIST POLITICAL THEORISTS

1
Feminism and political theory

Judith Evans

Preface

The argument of this chapter is two-fold. On the one hand, I seek to demonstrate that the essential techniques of political theorists are value-neutral, so that there is no intellectual reason why we cannot create a feminist perspective within political thought. On the other hand, I argue that political theorists should pay far more attention than they do to feminist writings. My basic aim is to convince the reader that no automatic distinction should be made between feminist writing and political theory; and that if the distinction continues to be made, political thought will be the victim.

When I speak of value neutrality, I do so not from a naïve assumption that no values are involved in the conduct of social science; nor do I claim that an easy distinction can be made between science and ideology. Rather, I believe that the bias exists in the assumptions of political theorists, but not in the techniques which they employ, which can be applied to feminist writings, and feminist concerns, as readily as they have been to other texts and issues.

While I have received valuable advice from colleagues on the drafting of this chapter, it should be emphasized that it cannot be regarded as the manifesto of the contributors to this book.

The aim of this chapter is to discuss the relationship between feminist writing and political theory:[1] to ask what, if anything, the former can add to the latter, to what extent it is capable of challenging its basic assumptions, and whether the two forms of discourse can coexist in any meaningful way. To this end, I shall review selected feminist works, ranging from discussions by academics of the depiction of women in classic texts of political thought, to writing – particularly in the radical feminist tradition – which would not normally be regarded as political or, perhaps, even theoretical, and would therefore most certainly be disregarded by mainstream political theory.

While there are deep and sometimes bitter ideological disagreements between feminists, any feminist is, at the very minimum, committed to some form of reappraisal of the position of women in society. Feminism, then, is avowedly not value-neutral, but politically engaged. It may not be immediately obvious to non-feminists, or other groups not interested in change except to oppose it, that political theory is itself so engaged; but insofar as it excludes or patronizes women (this is, of course, not the only charge that could be brought against it), it is. A consideration of the possibility of a *rapprochement* between feminism and political theory must, therefore, begin with one question: is the technique of theoretical inquiry, as opposed to its content and emphasis, value-free? Is it, that is, capable of embracing, inter alia, a feminist perspective? Or is there something inherent within it which ties it firmly to the derogation of women, and the defence of a male-dominated society?

I shall address this question not in abstraction from the subject matter of this chapter, but with reference to two feminist viewpoints which present the most radical challenge to political theory as we know it. Before this, however, a delineation of the current practice of the latter is necessary.[2] First, there is the task of textual exegesis: the outlining, discussion and interpretation of works of political thought such as Plato's *Republic,* Hobbes's *Leviathan*, and Rousseau's *The Social Contract*. (While there has been a certain concentration on such writers, more recent works are of course subject to similar analysis.) Second, there exists what might be termed a more conceptual approach: the clarification and elaboration of such ideas as rights, obligation, and consent. Third, philosophers such as Skinner (1979) have adopted a new way of appraising the classic literature, by placing it in its historical context. Fourth, there has occurred, some would argue, a revival of the classic tradition by thinkers such as Rawls (1972) and Nozick (1974), whose works have themselves inspired a new industry based on the first tendency discussed. Fifth, there has for some time existed a school of 'empirical', 'explanatory', or 'non-normative' theory: a varied enterprise, but one which as a rule seeks to produce law-like generalizations about politics and society. Sixth, political scientists engage in formal political analysis or mathematical political theory, concerned basically with model-building, though not of the type carried out by economists. Some would argue that there is a final category of thought, applied philosophy; but in fact this would seem to be a variant of the second tendency discussed, utilizing conceptual analysis in the discussion of, for example, medical ethics.

It can be seen that political theory is a wide ranging enterprise. It is therefore even more worthy of note than if the field were monolithic, that until relatively recently political theorists have had little or nothing to say about women. The disdain displayed by the classic works has been replaced by a stunning, but unnoticed silence. The tendencies in feminist thought to which I have alluded would regard this state of affairs as virtually if not, indeed, totally inevitable. It is on discussion of these tendencies that I shall rest my claim that this is not so; not so because technique, here regarded as comprising the first two tendencies within political theory outlined above, is value-neutral. The precise meaning of my claim will be stated in the argument that follows.

The first feminist tendency to be discussed is based on language and its uses; Spender's *Man Made Language* (1980)[3] is an exemplar of the viewpoint. The ultimate logic of the argument is that language defines, or expresses, the limits of our thought, and hence our world. The meanings our words bear both constitute, and are constituted by, our culture. Thus the use of 'he' and 'man' to include both male and female are not innocent linguistic conventions but, in a very important, though perhaps quasi-conscious, fashion, convey the message that in our society men are not merely more valuable than women, but are what society *is*: as it were, what society is all about. The political[4] component of such language use can indeed be very clearly seen in the controversy over the employment of such terms as chairman, chairwoman, chairperson and chair, and the derision to which, years after second-wave feminism began, those who seek to challenge the old terminology may be subjected. Apparently more directly relevant to my theme is a word such as 'politics'. However, given that its meaning is already interrogated by mainstream political science (Leftwich, ed., 1984), and indeed, as Lovenduski (1981: 86) has so well shown, political theory already contains a view of politics adaptable to feminist concerns,[5] I suggest that we are here faced not with a problem of insurmountable linguistic difficulty, but with a political battle to some extent already won. It is not the techniques of political theory that constitute an obstacle to change, but the attitudes of political theorists, dictating which definitions will be adopted, and the manner in which techniques will be applied.

The second feminist viewpoint in which I am interested is similar, for it too must concern itself with language; but it is far more intractable. This is the view that the experience of women, their enforced public 'silence' (Elshtain, 1981)[6] and their uniquely female values, may lead to a form of discourse which would be a different kind of political theory, unrecognizable as such. This view clearly derives from 'woman-centred' theory (Eisenstein, 1984). It demands the dethroning of logic and reason, and an acceptance of the postulate of woman's especial ties to nature; of those who do not share it, it requires a Kuhnian-style non-rational conversion (Kuhn, 1973: 89–91, 93–4) to a new paradigm or world view.

Of all accounts of the history and philosophy of science, Kuhn's would seem to come nearest to admitting the possibility not only of the existence but of the potential victory of a fully fledged woman-centred political theory. For Kuhn, the scientific enterprise consists in problem-solving, the problems being dictated by the reigning paradigm, during extensive periods of what is termed normal science (1973: chs III–V). However, these periods are punctuated by scientific revolutions (1973: ch. IX), such as the transition from Newtonian to Einsteinian physics, from one paradigm to another. Most importantly for my purposes, the scientist's conversion from one to another is not arrived at by a simple weighing of the evidence, but is a social and political act (1973: 89–91, 93–4, 151–2); though this may seem both too complex and too banal an account of a capitulation akin to Paul's on the road to Damascus. Highly relevant, also, is Kuhn's belief that successive paradigms are incommensurable one with another: cognitively, one cannot live simultaneously with the reigning view and its predecessor (1973: 147–50). Yet finally, scrutiny of the conduct of science forces us to say that Kuhn can offer the woman-centred school scant comfort; for after the conversion, the techniques of science at their most basic – the rules of evidence, logic, inference – remain.[7]

It should be said that it does not matter, for the purposes of my argument, whether Kuhn's account of the conduct of science is correct, unless both he and his opponents are wrong. As I have indicated, Kuhn's beliefs are, prima facie, by far the most favourable to the cause of a feminist revolution in thought; but in the end, even they do not support it. It should also be made clear that social scientists do not, on the whole, regard themselves as carrying out the same kind of enterprise as natural scientists. However, the objections to conflating the two processes of discovery – I shall mention here simply Hesse (1978), albeit she is not the most orthodox of protestors – do not rule out my account of the continuity of basic techniques, nor my use of Kuhn *as an analogy*, to aid my rejection of a school of thought which would jettison, wholesale, the methods of analysis we now employ.

In the case of political theory, then, what I am saying is that technique at its most basic, here defined as textual exegesis and conceptual analysis, is value-neutral: that it is the assumptions of the investigator, and the way they influence the use of technique, that are biased. Hence the postulation of woman-centred theory, as a replacement for the theory we now have, leads to a Humpty Dumpty world whose conditions we cannot accept. It must, however, be added that despite the fact that feminists of this persuasion are forced to share a common language with conventional theorists, their case is in an important sense quite literally unanswerable. The points that can be made against them spring, of course, from the very form of discourse they would regard as invalid. Logic, that is, is being used to defend itself against the avowedly non-logical. Even the most relentlessly mainstream feminist academic should feel a certain unease at this stage of the argument; the more so, the more she is aware of her socialization into the ways of academic thought.

With a lingering unhappiness, then, I shall propose that pending further developments I cannot now envisage, we should take the view that while feminism calls for a change in the content and emphasis of political theory – a consideration of feminist writings, direction or rather redirection of focus to, for example, the family, discussions of concepts such as love and compassion[8] – this can be accomplished without a change in technique. This is not to say that the enterprise, as I shall outline it below, will attain its goals with ease; there are powerful forces ranged against it. The point is that, purely from an intellectual viewpoint, there is no insuperable barrier to the acceptance by male theorists of the validity of a feminist perspective. Rather, their defences against it are psychological and political.

Indeed, it was the most basic of techniques, most conventionally used, which led to Okin's (1980) reappraisal of the treatment of women by political theorists from Plato to Mill. Okin's exposure of traditional attitudes to women is a welcome addition to mainstream analysis. If there is one basic argument in the book, it is that a functionalist justification, beginning with Aristotle and continuing today, has been used to legitimate the subordination of women. The book is problematic in two ways. Firstly – and not surprisingly, given the exclusion of a consideration of women from modern political thought – Okin is at a loss accurately to locate the twentieth-century heirs to the classic writers she re-reads. Secondly, her condemnation of functionalist thought is somewhat too wholesale. It is true – though this is not Okin's argument – that functionalism tends to a jigsaw view of society, assuming that because something exists, it must therefore have a particular societal function for existing. What is ill-conceived is Okin's view of functionalism as necessarily justifying, rather than explaining, the position of women; stripped of its normative connotations, an explanation of why the subordination of women is functional to a given society – assuming, that is, that the explanation is correct – is a most valuable weapon for feminism. This having been said, it must be acknowledged that Okin opened a door traditional theory has not managed to close: more works have followed, and they, like Okin's, are at least read by many male political theorists. (The actual impact of Okin's work is difficult to assess; its potential contribution, with that of its successors, is discussed below.)

Elshtain's (1981) more sophisticated work concentrates on the theme of the split between public and private in political theory. Again, she returns to the Greeks to begin her reconstruction of our theoretical heritage; again, though in a more integrated manner, she exposes the ways in which the classic authors have supported or rationalized women's oppression. Bolder than Okin, she turns, in considering the twentieth century, to feminist writing, using exactly the same type of analysis she brought to bear on earlier, male, writers.

Interesting and thought-provoking though Elshtain's discussion is, it is flawed at its very core. While belabouring all those who argue for an essential difference, be it biological or cultural, in the sexes' values, and modes of discourse and action, and yet also attacking those who believe that woman's persona might not be changed by her entry into the political realm as it currently exists, she resolutely, albeit implicitly, rejects the ideal of androgyny. Despite the inconsistencies which thus appear during the course of the book, this is not an impossible set of positions to hold, assuming that in each case it is the extreme form of the argument that is attacked. However, the book's conclusion both explains and highlights the problems of its earlier analysis: for Elshtain wishes to preserve the separation of the public and private realms, while creating an 'ethical polity' (1981: 351–3) suffused with the values of the latter. Here the analysis degenerates from its earlier sophistication; and moreover, as Siltanen and Stanworth have pointed out in their forthright attack (eds, 1984: 206), rests on a conservative and heterosexist view of a proper private life. It is further clear from the content and tone of the book's conclusion that Elshtain ultimately belongs to the school of thought that seeks to make the American pluralist garden lovely by a little judicious pruning, ignoring the resistance that attempts at radical reform would surely encounter. All things considered, feminism deserves more from a fine theorist than Hollywood sunsets.

It must now be asked what reappraisals such as Okin's and Elshtain's have added to the study of political thought. Clearly, the theorists they discuss will, with luck, be regarded in a new light; though it is difficult to avoid the depressing prognosis that, rather, those teachers who regard themselves as avant-garde will simply add to their courses a final class on Okin, and possibly Elshtain. While such ghettoizing is preferable to the apartheid of women's studies courses, it falls far short of a full acceptance of the importance of a feminist perspective on political theory. However, it has to be said that, despite their importance as pioneering works, Okin's conventionality of approach, and the somewhat cursory nature of Elshtain's discussion of modern feminist theory – as opposed for example to Eisenstein's (1984) – lend a certain credibility to such a reaction.

Pateman has carried her attack further into the enemy camp, via a mixture of exegesis and conceptual analysis. Articles such as 'Mere Auxiliaries to the Commonwealth: Women and the Origins of Liberalism' (Brennan and Pateman, 1979), while not directly locating contradictions within liberal theory, demonstrate the problems women pose for such theory. Furthermore, more ambitiously than the writers I have so far discussed, they begin to extend the argument into consideration of the links between liberalism and capitalism, and the consequences for women (and feminism) of the liberal individualist ideal. There is room here for the teacher to break the ghetto boundaries, given that the questions addressed are so fundamental; the question is whether s/he will.

The works I have so far discussed are mainstream in their approach, if not entirely – and most certainly not in the case of Pateman – in their political values. And with the work of Pateman, we are approaching the possibility of a vindication of my view that the techniques of political theory can fully be appropriated by feminists. However, with that partial exception, such works raise the question of what comprises a feminist perspective in political theory: whether silence should be addressed, as much as misogyny or ad hoc rationalizations of female subordination; and how far political theorists, female as well as male, can overcome their 'social amnesia' (Jacoby, 1977) to recapture their past, and reread their historically constituted present.

Two books which take the discussion further are *The Politics of Reproduction* (O'Brien, 1981), and *The Family in Political Thought* (Elshtain, ed., 1982). O'Brien provides both an overview of feminist and non-feminist thinkers, and political theory – an analysis of the political relevance of the changing conditions and status of biological reproduction – in its own right. The practical problem with this book is that theorists are likely to regard it as totally outside their purview – as 'feminist' rather than 'political' – and thus to banish it forever into women's studies programmes. In allowing and perpetuating so crude a distinction, they impoverish their enterprise both by the simple exclusion, and by the likely effect of pushing prudent feminist academics back to diligent exegesis of the egregious views of yet another earlier theorist – a project that cannot forever remain the sole approved feminist tendency within political theory.[9]

The importance of Elshtain's collection, for my purposes, is that it urges political theory towards a change in content and emphasis, reinstating the family as an important subject for political analysis. While the essays within it are written from a variety of theoretical perspectives, none of the approaches is likely to be totally intellectually unacceptable save to the most blinkered. A vital aspect of the book is that it is concerned not simply with the treatment of the family in political thought, but with what that treatment can tell us about the thinkers and traditions it interrogates. Another crucial aspect, for a feminist, is that it boldly discusses authors not normally admitted to the political pantheon: certain contemporary theorists (albeit briefly), Kafka, and Laing. Obviously the ability to do this depends on an unusually wide definition of politics; one not alien to political science (Dowse and Hughes, eds, 1972: 5–7), but frequently ignored. There is, for example, an essay on the politics of love (Glass, 1982). If books such as these make their way onto the reading lists of political theory courses, the cause of the feminist perspective will be greatly advanced.[10] (I do not ignore, nor regard with disdain, the fact that five male writers contributed to the book.)

Thus far, I have been concerned firstly with certain methodological issues, arguing that there is no essential incompatibility between feminism and political theory; and secondly, with academic works which have sought to reinstate women within political thought, and on occasion, challenged certain presuppositions of liberalism. I now turn to feminist theorists who, as Elshtain has pointed out,

> . . . have not felt constrained by the heavy legacy of the 'fathers' and thus have moved in more innovative directions than they might have otherwise.

It is important to note that Elshtain views this freedom as a liability, also, in that feminism has characteristically ignored, for example, the question of citizenship (1981: 202). It is tempting here to argue that citizenship of our political system is a nullity to these feminists; but it must be accepted not so much that second-wave feminism has not addressed itself to political questions, as that it has failed to provide a systematic interrogation of the concepts of politics and power. The theory that has emerged is, indeed, free from the heavy hand of political philosophy, its modes of discourse, and its fashions. It is innocent less of the fact that important male writers and male-constituted schools of thought exist, than of the 'necessity' to address particular questions, and to do so in a particular way. It is also true that various of the writings I shall discuss were born of anger and passion, are avowedly not value-free; it will later be argued that this does not disqualify them from being regarded as works of political theory, and further, that only a curiously naïve and amnesiac perspective could conclude that it did.

Firestone's *The Dialectic of Sex* (1971) is normally regarded as a major text of early radical feminism, because, as Spender (1985: 81) points out, it bears the 'hall-mark' by its insistence that the oppression of women and children is historically and analytically the foundation of all forms of oppression. Interestingly, she offers qualified praise to Marx and Engels for their historical materialism; she wishes to replace it by 'a materialist view of history based on sex itself' (Firestone, 1971: 6). Cultural variation is irrelevant, because a biologically-based dependence of child and woman on the adult male exists everywhere, and has always done so. Thus it is the biological difference between men and women (or rather, its cultural significance) that must be eliminated (1971: 9–11). This will occur via technological developments which may even make 'virgin birth' a possibility (1971: 223), though it should be noted that Firestone is well aware of the problems of technologies not subject to adequate control (1971: 233–4).

For Firestone,

> The problem becomes political . . . when one realizes that, although man is increasingly capable of freeing himself from the biological conditions that created his tyranny over women and children, he has little reason to want to give this tyranny up.

Thus a feminist revolution is essential; but it will not only free women and children from the cultural constraints currently imposed by biological difference, but eliminate all forms of class distinction and domination (1971: 10–12). (This parallels Marx's analysis, although Firestone does not spell out the comparison; the victory of the oppressed class, which itself comprises the negation of the social order, will bring about the end of the need for power relationships.) The new order would provide varied options for careers and personal life, with the exception of the nuclear family, based on formal ties and biological relationships, that we now know (1971: 256–74).

Firestone wrote in urgency and fury, and as she expected (1971: 225–6), was met with rage (Spender, 1985: 96). We do not know how she would view her book today. It must be said that it is difficult for a feminist electrified by *The Dialectic of Sex* when first published, re-reading it with a colder and more jaded eye, to appraise its potential contribution to political theory. It is, perhaps, not surprising that in speaking of Firestone both Spender (1985: 95) and Delmar (1979: 5) use the word 'despair', albeit Delmar's ultimate judgement (1979: 10), based on Firestone's emphasis on consciousness-raising, is that:

[consciousness-raising as revolutionary preparation] demands that the locus of women's oppression – the family and home – be discovered as a *political* institution, not just a *private* one . . . 'The personal is political' is an extremely effective slogan, since it is capable of many interpretations. One of the values of *The Dialectic of Sex* is that it demonstrates the course of an argument through which this thought could first appear: not as slogan, but as conclusion.

If Firestone had achieved this, then there would be no argument as to her relevance to political theory today. To my mind, she did not. The importance of her book lies rather in what is a major weakness in terms of coherence: the vast numbers of issues raised, most of which have been taken further by others. For example, Firestone raises the question of Freudianism and the sexism of neo-Freudian analysis, to be discussed more fully by Chesler (1972); the issue, following Ariès (1962), of the history of the creation of childhood and the subordination of children; the connection between racism and sexism, analysed by others, but not resolved; the creation, and oppressive character, of 'love' and 'romance'; the idea of technology as male and aesthetic as female;[11] and – this indeed merits further inquiry – the notion that technology informed by a feminist perspective could serve the interests of a radical ecology. (It should be emphasized that Firestone's analysis is politically a very hard-headed one, with no trace of romantic Luddism, or hymns to woman and nature.) It is not, then, merely as a historical document, or a utopia, that Firestone deserves our attention today.

Millett's *Sexual Politics* (1972) is a very different work, both in content – a study of the politics of sexuality largely via literature – and in style, presumably because of its initial incarnation as a doctoral thesis. *Qua* thesis, Millett's central perception is the ubiquity of an imagery of power and (frequently violent, even sadistic) domination in male writing about sex, and the exposure of the structure of sexual dominance in Genet's accounts of homosexuality (Millett, 1972: chs 1, 5–8). The less literary sections of the book are Chapter Two – which stands as a feminist and political analysis in its own right – and Part II. The importance of the second chapter, entitled 'Theory of Sexual Politics', lies in the clarity and care of its language (for example, 'politics' is clearly defined as 'power-structured relationships' (1972: 23)), and in the fact that, *pace* the critics of radical feminism, it is categorically stated that patriarchy takes many forms (1972: 25–6), and there is a suggestion that it should be regarded as an ideal type. The book as a whole (though especially Part II, 'Historical Background') is a remarkable synthesis of historical, sociological, anthropological, scientific and literary sources and arguments, displaying a richness of insight that defies summary. If there is one feminist work that should persuade us that we live in a patriarchal culture, it is *Sexual Politics*; its felicity is to make the point with erudition, while avoiding endless statistical recital. All who seek to understand revolt and revolution should read the discussion of Genet (Millett, 1972: ch. 8, esp. 349–61). Insofar as Millett presents us with a theory that is political, there is little if any need to justify the study of her work by political scientists. I end my discussion with the final words of the introductory chapter (referring to Genet):

> The brothel will open again tomorrow for an identical ritual. The sounds of revolution begin again offstage but unless the Police Chief is permanently imprisoned in his tomb and unless the new rebels have truly forsworn the customary idiocy of the old sexual politics, there will be no revolution. . . .unless we eliminate the most pernicious of our systems of oppression, unless we go to the very center of the sexual politic and its sick delirium of power and violence, all our efforts at liberation will only land us again in the same primordial stews. (1972: 22)

As Spender (1985: 155) has pointed out,

> Until about 1972 it would have been possible for some people to claim to have read *all* the contemporary feminist books: after 1972 such a claim would have become increasingly absurd.

Thus, while for practical reasons I have omitted from my account Greer's *The Female Eunuch* (1971),[12] Chesler's *Women and Madness* (1972), and Brownmiller's *Against Our Will* (1976),[13] henceforward omissions must be explained by the impossibility of producing a comprehensive survey of the 'knowledge explosion' (Spender, 1985: 155), and distortion by the problem that it may not be the most important or the most representative writing that is most generally available to the researcher.

From around 1972, as Spender (1985; 159–61) and Eisenstein (1984: 47) would agree, feminist and more especially radical feminist writing has increasingly consisted in and advocated a woman-centred perspective, insisting on grounding feminist analysis in female experience[14] and challenging male-constituted understandings of meaning and knowledge. I have already suggested that, at its extreme, this school of thought posits an enterprise incompatible with political theory, and one whose claims to a superior form of knowledge we must reject. Nevertheless, as I do not agree with Eisenstein (1984: 135) that such writing is necessarily to be regarded as 'a metaphysical or spiritual journey, rather than a political one', I shall give such indication as I can of what the school is saying.

The title of Daly's *Gyn/Ecology* (1978) gives some idea of the nature of her work. Like Cixous (1981: 90), she is concerned to 'deconstruct' conventional language, and modes of thought; like

Gauthier (1981: 199), to discard the persona we have adopted,[15] and celebrate woman as witch. Stylistically, her work, like that of Griffin (1978), departs from the conventional in its mixture of neologism, prose-poetry, and prose purple beyond measure; and politically, returns to a 1960s view of withdrawal from the conventional world, but this time in an even more accentuated form.

Eisenstein (1984: 125) argues that, despite the adoption of the woman-centred perspective, there are three important elements within contemporary radical feminism that also existed in the early writings:

> . . . (1) a divorce from the left and from Marxism; (2) a focus on psychology at the expense of economics; and (3) a false universalism in the analysis of gender.

I discuss in my later chapter the disillusion with the male left of which Eisenstein also writes. Her view (1984: 128–9) is that while socialist feminism remains as yet a tentative enterprise, still, and especially in the political climate of the 1980s, to abandon questions of capitalism and class is to give the ideological terrain over to the enemy. The 'focus on psychology' is disliked by Eisenstein because the politics of the personal are not sufficiently linked to wider issues of social, economic and macro-political power and oppression, and because the school

> may have given many women the impression that in order to transform their situation, it sufficed to change the way they thought about the world. (1984: 131)

The final point concerns the extrapolation of the insight that whatever their background, women have much in common, to a dogma that all women face the same oppression in the same form (Eisenstein 1984: 132–5). (Women of colour, for so long absent from second-wave feminism, have now of course challenged the preoccupations of middle-class whites, and third world women have forcefully pointed out, at international meetings, that for them a concern with the personal is a luxury, if not an irrelevance.)

I have documented the continuities seen by Eisenstein between early radical feminism and its present-day representatives. The first is inherent in the radical feminist project; the second ill-conceived, in my view, only to the extent that it is divorced from other forms of analysis; the third an understandable tendency given the notion of patriarchy, but a betrayal of the early androgynous perspective. But Eisenstein also perceives an important discontinuity between early and current radical feminism, in the shift from an emphasis on radical change to a withdrawal from the public/political (1984: 136).

I find myself in considerable agreement with Eisenstein's

argument, in many ways; but regard as dubious her characterization of woman-centred analysis as non-political. Elsewhere, I have expressed reservations about the political implications of analogous beliefs (Evans, 1980: 112). But to call them non-political, rather than, as I believe to be the case, potentially demobilizing, and reactionary, is to ignore two important factors. Firstly, on a wider definition of politics than that normally employed, but nevertheless, one that is in principle accepted by political scientists, they are political insofar as they address the existence of domination and the exercise of power. Secondly, despite reservations one might feel about the overall character and results of Daly's project, it is clear that she has the power to politicize,[16] albeit that power must be sustained and extended by the work of others.

Further, Eisenstein's alternative proposal, given the general sophistication of her analysis, is sadly simplistic: to bring our grievances into 'politics' by campaigns on, for example, child care and health (1984: 144). If we are not to end with more confused, divisive, and weary campaigns on, say, pornography,[17] then we must attempt, rather, the difficult task of unifying various forms of theory, connecting the micro- and macro-political, in a way that has not yet been done. Finally, Eisenstein's attack on anger as a motivating force (1984: 129) not only devalues the suffering of at least one generation of women,[18] but ignores the fact that, while in academic analysis one may strive for impartiality, anger, justified and understood, is no bad lever for social and intellectual change.

There remains the question of the relationship of the writers I have discussed to political theory. With the possible exception of the members of the woman-centred school, their acceptance *as* political theorists, and as proper subjects for analysis by academics, is long overdue. They have re-characterized society, and rehabilitated, as components of political discussion, the family, sexuality, patriarchy newly defined, and other feminist concerns. They may not conform, in style, to the tenets of political philosophy; but to suggest that they should, is to bestow on that field a stasis the classic writers, themselves, would one hopes have rejected; and certainly to forget that they were both men of their time, and innovators. If there is one school of thought that brings new life and a new vision to social and political theory, it is feminism; this alone gives us warrant to suggest that the automatic and unreflecting distinction between feminist writing and political theory be forgone.

I do not demand the immediate entry of these works into the accepted corpus of the history of political thought: that is far too immodest a proposal. And yet, such an acceptance might be the only foundation, via the dialectical process of teaching and research, for their eventual uniting. Otherwise feminist writings will continue to be seen, by the vast majority of academics, as neither theoretical nor political. As I have argued when discussing them, this is wrong.

I referred, earlier, to those who would exclude feminist writing from the corpus of political theory because of the anger and commitment of the former, as being possessed of a 'curiously naïve and amnesiac perspective'. What I mean, here, is that a field of study which can accommodate, for example, Rousseau and Marx is in no position to rule out writers because of their openly avowed values. Nor, because it is now the fashion to cast a cold eye, should we assume that anger is allowed only to voices from the past.

In writing this chapter, I encountered a certain unease in confronting Firestone, not as an inspiration of my feminist youth, but as an object of academic analysis. Spender, who approaches these matters rather differently, nevertheless appears to have encountered something of the same problem in re-reading Greer (Spender, 1985: 48–50). Thus a feminist re-reading *of* feminism poses problems alien to those who, in the emotionally if not always intellectually tranquil tradition of the history of thought, interrogate writers such as Hobbes and Locke. Thus the fear of confronting emotion may prove part of the psychological barrier, albeit very probably an unconscious one, which I have already suggested is part of the main obstacle to the acceptance of a feminist perspective in political theory. If it can be overcome, then we may indeed, though not in the manner suggested by the woman-centred school, succeed in creating a political theory of a new kind.

Notes

I am grateful to Jill Hills, Joni Lovenduski and Ursula Vogel for their comments on an earlier draft of this chapter. The views expressed here are, of course, my own.

1. It will be seen that this is a distinction that, at least in its normal automatic and unreflective form, I reject. However, I have thought it better to retain the dichotomy in my writing, for clarity of exposition.

2. I have omitted Marxism, and with it Marxist feminism, as my major concern is with mainstream, and therefore liberal, political theory.

3. See the extended review of Spender by Assiter (1985).

4. By 'political' I mean here power-based and conflictual action.

5. The reference is to Wolin's (1961: 5) view of 'politics' as a social construct.

6. Elshtain is, of course, not a proponent of the view I am outlining.

7. I derive this view not from the vast secondary literature on Kuhn, but from discussions with political theorists and practising scientists with an interest in the history and philosophy of science.

8. While I do not personally believe that women are more loving or compassionate than men, I am convinced by the nature of the available literature that feminism would indeed tend towards an emphasis on such concerns.

9. Pateman's rather different approach is, of course, also accepted. I take it to be a

sign of the high esteem in which she is generally held, as well as of the quality of her work in this area, that this is so.

10. I do not mean to suggest that there is one correct perspective on political theory, but rather that the various approaches present a unity in opposition to non-feminist readings.

11. There is a problem here – though not that faced by those who postulate such a difference as inherent – in that Firestone appears to hover between the position that these characteristics are dictated by sex (biology), and a milder proposition that they are constructs of the social system of gender.

12. It is also true that I do not believe that *The Female Eunuch*, in its day a polemic of great power, has anything of significance to offer us now.

13. See the analyses of these writings in Eisenstein (1984) and Spender (1985). (While Brownmiller would seem to belong to a later school, I have no hesitation in placing her with the theorists of 1970.)

14. There is, of course, an arrogance and elitism here: who is to decide on what will count as bona fide female experience?

15. Or the persona which has been forced upon us.

16. This view emerges from my experience as a teacher.

17. I am not suggesting that such campaigns are totally without merit but, rather, arguing that their production is very far from being the ultimate task of feminism.

18. This is not to say that women have not always suffered. What I am pointing to is the particular disillusion and anger felt by the first generation of second-wave feminists.

References

Ariès, P. (1962) *Centuries of Childhood*. London: Jonathan Cape.

Assiter, A. (1985) 'Did Man Make Language', pp. 310–21 in R. Edgley and R. Osborne (eds), *Radical Philosophy Reader*. London: Verso.

Brennan, T. and C. Pateman (1979) 'Mere Auxiliaries to the Commonwealth', *Political Studies*, XXVII(2): 183–200.

Brownmiller, S. (1976) *Against Our Will*. Harmondsworth: Penguin.

Chesler, P. (1972) *Women and Madness*. London: Allen Lane.

Cixous, H. (1981) 'Sorties', pp. 90–98 in E. Marks and I. de Courtivron (eds), *New French Feminisms*. Brighton: Harvester.

Daly, M. (1978) *Gyn/Ecology*. London: The Women's Press.

Delmar, R. (1979) 'Introduction' to S. Firestone, *The Dialectic of Sex*. London: The Women's Press.

Dowse, R. and J. Hughes (eds) (1972) *Political Sociology*. London: Wiley.

Eisenstein, H. (1984) *Contemporary Feminist Thought*. London: Unwin Paperbacks.

Elshtain, J. (1981) *Public Man, Private Woman*. Oxford: Martin Robertson.

Elshtain, J. (ed.) (1982) *The Family in Political Thought*. Brighton: Harvester.

Evans, J. (1980) 'Attitudes to Women in American Political Science', *Government and Opposition*, 15(1): 101–41.

Firestone, S. (1971) *The Dialectic of Sex*. London: Jonathan Cape (first published 1970).

Gauthier, X. (1981) 'Existe-t-il une écriture de femme?', pp. 161–4 in E. Marks and I. de Courtivron (eds), *New French Feminisms*. Brighton: Harvester.

Glass, J. (1982) 'Kafka and Laing on the Trapped Consciousness', pp. 269–87 in J. Elshtain (ed.), *The Family in Political Thought*. Brighton: Harvester.

Greer, G. (1971) *The Female Eunuch*. London: Paladin.

Griffin, S. (1978) *Woman and Nature*. New York: Harper & Row.

Hesse, M. (1978) 'Theory and Value in the Social Sciences', pp. 1–16 in C. Hookway and P. Pettit (eds), *Action and Interpretation*. Cambridge: Cambridge University Press.

Jacoby, R. (1977) *Social Amnesia*. Brighton: Harvester.

Kuhn, T. (1973) *The Structure of Scientific Revolutions*. Chicago and London: The University of Chicago Press.

Leftwich, A. (ed.) (1984) *What is Politics?* Oxford: Blackwell.

Lovenduski, J. (1981) 'Toward the Emasculation of Political Science', pp. 83–97 in D. Spender (ed.), *Men's Studies Modified*. Oxford: Pergamon.

Millett, K. (1972) *Sexual Politics*. London: Abacus (first published 1970).

Nozick, R. (1974) *Anarchy, State and Utopia*. Oxford: Blackwell.

O'Brien, M. (1981) *The Politics of Reproduction*. London: Routledge.

Okin, S. (1980) *Women in Western Political Thought*. London: Virago (first published 1979).

Rawls, J. (1972) *A Theory of Justice*. Oxford: Clarendon Press.

Siltanen, J. and M. Stanworth (eds) (1984) *Women and the Public Sphere*. London: Hutchinson.

Skinner, Q. (1979) *Foundations of Modern Political Thought*. Vol. I, *The Renaissance*. Cambridge: Cambridge University Press.

Spender, D. (1980) *Man Made Language*. London: Routledge.

Spender, D. (1985) *For the Record*. London: The Women's Press.

Wolin, S. (1961) *Politics and Vision*. London: Allen & Unwin.

II

THE HISTORICAL PERSPECTIVE

2

Rationalism and romanticism: two strategies for women's liberation

Ursula Vogel

A wild wish has just flown from my heart to my head, and I will not stifle it, though it may excite a horse-laugh. I do earnestly wish to see the distinction of sex confounded in society. (M. Wollstonecraft)

What could be uglier than exaggerated femininity, what more repulsive than exaggerated masculinity as they prevail in our morals and opinions today? . . . Only *self-reliant femininity* and *gentle masculinity* should be called good and beautiful. (Friedrich Schlegel)

Preface

I first came to be interested in the eighteenth-century debate on women's emancipation as a particular instance in a broader framework of philosophical and historical questions directed at the political implications and the internal consistency of the Enlightenment's belief in individual autonomy. To what extent was the postulated universal link between moral autonomy, political right and democratic citizenship actualized with regard to various groups hitherto excluded from full participation in the community? In what direction would not only political institutions but also personal and social relationships have to change in order to make it possible for all individuals – defined and divided by religion, race, class and sex – to exercise their right to self-determination?

On closer examination it became apparent that the attempt to extend to women the freedom ascribed to all autonomous agents faced obstacles of a particular and unique kind. Discrimination against women differed from the treatment suffered by other underprivileged groups in the eighteenth century (such as Jews, Blacks, or the poor) in that the reasons for exclusion cannot easily be rendered transparent. They are sunk in, and obscured by, personal relations which resist identification as forms of domination and subjugation. Thus the position and roles of men and women within the private sphere of the family appeared, even to those radical thinkers most

17

anxious to expose the conventional character of all institutions, as the embodiment of natural, immutable differences.

The contradictions which entered into the arguments of eighteenth-century advocates of women's independence, as they sought to locate the conditions of emancipation between the two poles of an undifferentiated human nature and a particular gender identity, confront the historian of political thought with difficult and embarrassing questions. Not only do they demonstrate a failure of practical consistency – a failure to apply indiscriminately the universal principles which underlie liberal and democratic values – they also cast doubt upon the claimed universality of these basic moral principles themselves. That is to say, one is led to ask whether already on the most abstract philosophical level concepts such as liberty, right, justice, or citizenship do not contain an in-built bias against the full inclusion of women – so that their exclusion cannot simply be disposed of as an oversight or as an inconsistency explicable in terms of specific historical, that is contingent, factors.

It is not my intention to make claims for a special feminist methodology in the history of political thought to be set against the conventional standards of conceptual analysis and historical explana- tion. (I agree with Judy Evans's view, expounded in the introductory chapter of this volume, that the methodological foundations of political theorizing must be considered as value – and sex-neutral.) But it can be shown that the specific issue of women's subordination and liberation raises a whole range of new questions and sheds new light upon the limitations and inconsistencies and – equally – upon the radical potential inherent in the liberal tradition of political theory.

This latter point, too, deserves emphasis and can provide a corrective to an overly simple reading of the history of political thought by feminists today. From the viewpoint of the present the inadequacies of early feminist thinking may seem all too obvious. The abstract and exalted individualism manifest in the understanding of freedom and self-determination, the narrow focus on changes in the legal and political superstructure and, most significantly, the failure to break with the traditional separation between the public and the private sphere impeded a full recognition of the informal mechanisms at the root of women's subjugation and of the collective character of their inferior position. Although it is true that we do not find in eighteenth-century arguments an understanding of the pervasive structures of patriarchal domination developed in contem- porary feminist writings, it is also true that they do not fit the stereotype of a typical 'liberal' or 'bourgeois' ideology (under which these shortcomings are often listed). I argue in this chapter that both the rationalist and the romantic cases for women's liberation transcend these ideological confines and that in general the history of political thought must be open to a differentiated and discriminating reading by feminists today.

One way of describing the major differences and cleavages within contemporary feminist thinking is to apply to them the philosophical and historical categories by which we commonly distinguish between the political doctrines of Liberalism, Socialism and Marxism. However, some of the most characteristic and most impassionately argued divisions in the present debate among feminists cut across these familiar ideological boundaries. They can perhaps best be summarized in the contrast between a political and an aesthetic conception of women's liberation. Stated in a simplified form: whereas the former aims at ending women's oppression by political means (through changes in the legal and institutional structure of society), the latter is committed to a strategy of revolutionizing the very basis of personal experiences and intimate relationships, at the expense, so it may seem, of a retreat from politics (see Sichtermann, 1983: 102–13; Jaggar, 1983: 254ff.).

At issue here is not merely a different ranking of strategic priorities or disagreement about the most effective means to achieve the same end. Rather, the two strategies highlight a more fundamental difference concerning the ways in which we should perceive women's *specific* identity in relation to the *universal* concepts of human nature, reason, morality, rights and citizenship.

In this chapter, I will examine a contrast of similar dimensions in the eighteenth-century debate on women. In the term 'rationalism', I shall refer to the emphasis on those universal and uniform features in individual human beings which are owed to the faculty of reason. In relation to rational agency, as the essential attribute of human nature, differences of sex – like those of racial, ethnic or national character – are considered as having no relevance. Politically, the rationalist argument – which is represented here by Condorcet, Mary Wollstonecraft and the German Jacobin Theodor von Hippel – aims at the inclusion of women in the 'Rights of Man' postulated in the democratic constitutions of the French Revolution: a fundamental change in women's public status based upon their recognition as the fellow citizens of men must be the first step and prime lever in the process of their emancipation.[1]

By contrast, 'romanticism', as it first developed in Germany in the closing decade of the eighteenth century, stands for an aesthetic ideal of the many-faceted human personality in whom all faculties – reason and feeling, spirituality and sensuality – are fully and harmoniously developed.[2] Since in its perception of beauty and truth romantic thinking places diversity above uniformity and the particular and original above the dictates of universal norms, it must assign value also to the differentiations and the polarity of sexual character. These preconceptions underlie the romantic strategy of women's liberation which is directed towards the goal of 'independent femininity'. In its political implications this goal, with its acceptance of the gender-specific characteristics of human nature, should not be mistaken for a mere conservative endorsement of women's special status in civil society. Rather, the romantic position differs from the rationalist mainly in that it considers the political sphere as altogether marginal to the experiences and endeavours through which individuals (men as well as women!) can realize their truly human potential. Not 'rational fellowship' among citizens, but romantic love freed from the confines of conventional sexual roles points towards the utopia of a regenerated world.

In the texts under discussion here, all of which stem originally from the 1790s (Condorcet, 1976a; von Hippel, 1977; Wollstonecraft, 1975; Schlegel, 1983; Schlegel, 1964; and Schleiermacher, 1964), the reflection on the condition of women is not a matter of peripheral concern. It occupies the centre both of philosophical argument and of historical theorizing. These authors recognize that the prevailing beliefs about women, if left unchallenged, threaten to undermine the major presumptions of modern political thinking. Nothing less is at stake than the general validity of the principles associated with natural right, moral autonomy and democratic legitimacy. Similarly, the issue of women's subordination serves as a catalyst for the sharper perception of the specific contradictions of modern civilization. It testifies to the fragility of intellectual and moral progress by highlighting an area which has remained almost completely resistant to modern notions of freedom. The emphasis here is different: while the rationalist associates the oppression of women, and the defects of present society in general, with the all-pervasive effects of social and political inequality, the romantic critic focuses on the hypocrisy and pettiness of bourgeois philistine morality in which he sees the most telling signs of the profound corruption of modern culture.

Both perspectives converge in a common polemical purpose – to refute the ideas of Rousseau, 'the pharisee of our times' (von Hippel, 1977: 40; see also Schlegel, 1983: 129; Wollstonecraft, 1975: 127) who, it is claimed, has done more than any other modern philosopher to lend to blatant prejudice against women the false dignity of profound truth. With regard to this polemical target, rationalists and romantics are at one in their opposition to any form of biological reductionism. They deny, that is, the validity of assumptions according to which the capacities of women and their role in civil society should be defined by the allegedly immutable dictates of physical nature.

In opposing this narrowly deterministic account by the assertion of women's capacity for freedom the rationalist and the romantic critique follow different routes and draw upon different assumptions. My comparison of these two strategies for liberation will concentrate on the following issues and questions. First, is the centrality of reason to the claims made for women's independence. Can the demand for moral and political self-determination accommodate significant gender-specific differences in rationality? Which role may be attributed to the passions, especially those associated with erotic desire and love? Second, which form of personal and public relationships between women and men will guarantee the postulate of equal freedom? Third, what is the relevance of *political* liberation for the *human* emancipation of women?

The logic of natural right
'Either no individual of the human species has any true rights, or all have the same' (Condorcet, 1976a: 98).

The article, 'On the Admission of Women to the Rights of Citizenship', was written in 1790 by Condorcet, himself a member of the French National Assembly, with the aim of moving his fellow revolutionaries to adopt a more enlightened attitude towards women. The argument formed part of his radical conception of a rational political order based upon complete equality between the sexes with regard to both political rights and educational opportunities (see Baker, 1976).

In less than ten pages the article scrutinizes and demolishes the then prevailing views on the proper role and sphere of women in civil society. It reflects, in an exemplary fashion, the attitude of the Enlightenment *philosophe* who seeks to break the power of oppressive institutions by unveiling the web of hidden errors and unexamined beliefs from which they draw legitimacy. Condorcet recognizes that the position of women is unique in comparison with that of other oppressed groups in that the violation of their rights has so far gone largely unnoticed. There can be no stronger proof of the power of prejudice over people's minds than the fact that we may hear, even among the most enlightened and benevolent reformers, 'the principle of equality invoked in favour of 300 or 400 men . . . and forgotten in the case of some 12 million women' (Condorcet, 1976a: 98).

He contends that there is not a single sound reason why women should not be included in the rights which the French Revolution has claimed on behalf of all human beings. It would be impossible to maintain that women do not possess the same rights as men without attacking the very foundations of the rights claim itself, which is based simply upon the existence of 'sentient beings who are capable of acquiring moral ideas and of reasoning' (1976a: 98). Any special pleading, any appeal to the particular characteristics, significant differences and alleged inferiorities of the female sex must invariably call into question the basic principles of a democratic constitution.

Equally conclusive is the refutation of what may at first sight seem a stronger reason for political discrimination – namely that women, although in principle entitled to rights, as yet lack the capacity and competence of active political participation. Simple logic, Condorcet claims, at once reveals the absurdity of such opinion: if physical disabilities, such as passing indispositions and pregnancies, are to weigh against the exercise of civic rights, why has nobody dreamt of withholding them 'from persons who have the gout all winter or catch cold quickly' (1976a: 98)? Similarly, a situation which ties women to a daily routine of absorbing tasks cannot be held to disqualify them from engaging in public affairs, since this same condition applies to all male citizens who do not live a life of complete leisure. To make political rights dependent on special knowledge and trained exercise of reason (which women – like the majority of men 'occupied in constant labour' – have so far had little opportunity to develop) would strike at the very heart of a free constitution:

> Soon, little by little, only persons who had taken a course in public law would be permitted to be citizens. If such principles are admitted, we must, as a natural consequence, renounce any idea of a free constitution. The various aristocracies have had nothing but similar pretexts as their foundation or excuse . . . (1976a: 100)

In pursuing the logic inherent in the principle of natural right, Condorcet exposes the self-righteous and hypocritical attitude of men who attribute to women natural disabilities which are but the result of misdirected education and of previous legal discrimination continually reproduced. He reveals the vicious circle of reasoning so often deployed by defenders of the status quo in order to fend off the claims of hitherto disadvantaged groups:

> It is therefore unjust to allege, as an excuse for continuing to refuse women the enjoyment of their natural rights, grounds which have only a kind of reality because women do not exercise these rights. (1976a: 100)

No less important for the strategy of emancipation is his attempt (similar to the one undertaken by Paine in *The Rights of Man*) to demystify and democratize 'reason' and thus to withdraw the spurious legitimacy from the most common assertions of women's inferiority. Reason consists in nothing but the effective pursuit of those goals which human beings have learnt to consider important for their happiness: 'It is as reasonable for a woman to concern herself with her personal attractions as it was for Demosthenes to cultivate his voice and gestures' (1976a: 100). In its wider implications this argument sheds light upon a sensitive problem which was much in evidence in democratic theorizing of this time. The exclusion of women from the vote – like that of the poor or of ethnic minorities – raised difficult questions about the nature and conditions of democratic citizenship. On the one hand, the advocates of democracy subscribed to the view that all individuals should, merely by virtue of their equal natural rights, be entitled to political rights. On the other hand, however, most of them demanded certain qualifications (most commonly property) as proof of civic competence for the actual admission to rights of political participation. With regard to women, this inconsistency was particularly striking since their exclusion could not in all cases be justified on economic grounds and thus had to be defended in terms of natural disabilities, such as inferior reason, enslavement to the passions, and so on. The salient point here is that for women the demands on reason were raised above the level of ordinary rationality or common sense normally deemed sufficient for the entitlement to political rights (see Green, 1976).

Finally, Condorcet's critique strikes at the heart of the revolutionary ideology. Indeed, this is its main target. He shows how the most radical opponents of monarchical despotism and aristocratic privilege are themselves still the prisoners of prejudice who will ignore or even explicitly endorse the despotic power exercised by men over women (see Graham, 1977).

From a feminist viewpoint today the limits of this radicalism might be inferred from the belief that motherhood and 'a more retiring, more domestic life' are natural to women and will not be greatly affected by a change in their legal status. Condorcet concedes that, due to these natural preoccupations, they will be less likely *actually* to engage in political affairs (for instance by standing for elections) than men. His main concern is to ensure for them the dignity and self-respect which depends upon, and is satisfied by, the public recognition of their equal rights. Like Mary Wollstonecraft, he sees the most beneficial effects of this equality in the improvements of human relations within the family:

> And so it is unnecessary to believe that because women could become members of national assemblies they would immediately abandon their children, their homes and their needles. They would only be better fitted to educate their children and to rear men . . . Gallantry would doubtless

lose by the change, but domestic relations would be improved in this as in other things. (Condorcet, 1976a: 102)

These last arguments suggest that Condorcet's demand for women's equality is still constrained by the traditional separation of the private from the public sphere. However, we should not overlook the elements of a utopian vision characteristic of political egalitarianism in this time. The utopia appears in the hope that equality of right – the public recognition of women as citizens – far from being only a formal entitlement – will bring about a fundamental transformation in all relations between the members of a democratic society:

> Up to this time the manners of all known peoples have been brutal or corrupt . . . Up to this time, among all peoples, legal inequality has existed between men and women; and it would not be difficult to prove that, in these two equally general phenomena, the second is one of the principal causes of the first. For inequality necessarily introduces corruption, and is its most common (if not even its sole) cause. (1976a: 102)

The origins of inequality between women and men
In von Hippel (the rather uncommon case of a Prussian bureaucrat with Jacobin leanings) we encounter one of the most radical statements ('On the Civil Improvement of Women', 1977, originally published 1793) of women's equality which is not merely asserted on moral and political grounds but extended to the sphere of natural biological differences. Whereas Condorcet and Mary Wollstonecraft concede inequality of physical constitution while refuting its moral and intellectual relevance, here the rationalist critique of irrelevant differences approaches the near complete assimilation of femaleness and maleness in a genderless conception of human nature. Given the enormous significance which the defenders of women's subordination attributed to their inferiority of bodily strength and to their incapacitation through pregnancy and childbirth, it may have seemed necessary to von Hippel to question even this seemingly incontestable natural basis of common prejudice.

He examines even the innermost sanctuary of 'natural' inequality between women and men associated with the production and rearing of offspring in terms of usurped power and imposed inferiority, and denies that the common division of labour within the family is in any way sanctioned by nature or compatible with reason. Reducing all gender-specific characteristics to minor anatomic variations, with no significant impact on strength or frailty of bodily constitution, he pays no tribute to the notion of femininity, not even to motherhood: women's present biological nature is mostly the product of culture, more specifically, the artefact of men (see von Hippel, 1977: chs. 2 and 3).

To substantiate this claim he sketches a conjectural history of civilization reconstructed on a materialist basis: '*where, when* and *how* did the superior power of man over woman come into being? Which forces put the sword into the hand of man while consigning woman to the spinning wheel?' (1977: 51). Von Hippel argues that the now observable fact of woman's physical dependence and submissiveness must have evolved already in the earliest stages of human associations – from some cause which induced women to provide for their offspring and other domestic needs at home while leaving to men the activities of hunting and fishing. The point here is that this division of labour cannot have been necessary, that is, not have been the inevitable effect of pregnancy and childbirth. Childbirth as such is not debilitating. Nor need it interfere with a woman's ability to perform the same physical labour as a man – a fact amply demonstrated by the condition of women in the labouring classes who shoulder the double burden of hard work and domestic drudgery. The delicacy of female constitution to be found among the ladies of high society is a curse of civilization rather than of nature (1977: 30–4). The division of labour between domestic and outdoor tasks may have arisen from an unfortunate attention on the part of women to the security of future provisions which led them to cumulate food and domesticate animals, until they finally abandoned any activities outside the house. It was as a consequence of these regrettable – and avoidable – developments that men, bearing weapons and steeling body and mind in a world of wider experience, could gradually establish a position of superiority. Untrained in the use of weapons and lacking the opportunities of developing bodily strength, women *became* afraid of physical dangers and willing to submit to the predatory power of men.

> As woman took command over domestic animals she soon became one herself . . . Surrounded by petty objects and by beasts who patiently submitted to bridle and yoke woman gradually sank, in body and mind, to a lower station. (1977: 60)

With the institution of civil society every step in civilization widened the gulf and consolidated the power of men over their domestic slaves.

This rather amusing account – which culminates in the charge that women's subjugation must ultimately be blamed on the aggressive nature of hunting – can hardly claim the credentials of accurate history. Nor is it intended as such. Fragments of evidence concerning primitive society, psychological observations, analogies with the condition of slavery and the Kantian postulate of autonomy – all these disparate elements serve as building blocks in a philosophical and moral critique of women's condition in modern society. This philosophical reconstruction of history, revealing the sequence of causes that must have led to women's subordination, can be seen to perform important functions in the rationalist strategy of emancipation. It also highlights some of its inadequacies, explained below.

First, von Hippel wants to demonstrate that the indisputable observable inequalities between the sexes are not rooted in, and sanctioned by, nature. Femininity in all its aspects must be shown as a product of civilization. Nothing but uniformity of biological, mental and normal character, so it seems, can effectively underwrite the claim to equal rights. From the romantic perspective, this assumption will be denounced as symptomatic of the poverty of rationalism: in order to assert the equal worth of individuals the latter has to reduce diversity to the bland and empty abstractions of identical human nature.

Second, philosophical history can pierce the 'intricate spider's web of casuistic reasoning whereby we condemn the female sex to perpetual tutelage' (von Hippel, 1977: 69). It seeks to explain why from an original basis of natural equality women's condition could have developed in such a way that their subjection now appears natural. Von Hippel stresses the fatal dynamic inherent in the spiral of social inequality. Once the first and imperceptible steps in the division of labour had occurred the gap between the sexes was continuously reproduced and enlarged, both in the institutions of civil society and in the mental and moral state of individuals. Thus after women became tied exclusively to the tasks of the domestic sphere – a sphere of much narrower experience than that occupied by men – their capacities and energies gradually attuned themselves to its limited demands. Their development could not keep pace with that of their companions until it did, indeed, appear as if they were not at all equipped for exercising rights and responsibilities in the public domain (a condition further exacerbated by legal and political discrimination) (1977: 79f.).

Third, to identify the real historical causes in what is taken to be a perennial natural condition allows us to assign responsibility – to the male sex collectively. Women themselves, von Hippel claims, are not implicated in the process of their subjugation; they have lost their position and rights as the equals of men through no fault of their own. In this respect he seems to anticipate some of the arguments about 'patriarchy' current in radical feminism today (see Jaggar, 1983: 255–69). He moves beyond, and radicalizes, the typical Enlightenment emphasis on the power of prejudice by insisting that the latter is but a thin facade for naked coercive power exercised by men over women and supported by the brutality of civil laws.

Fourth, if one can discern, in the vast distance which separates women's position in civilized society from their nature, an intelligible causal pattern of historical development, it is then possible to show how its effects might be corrected by rational political action. Equality of rights (including access to public office) and, equally important, education of male and female children towards the uniform status of citizens can, Hippel believes, undo the relations of power and subjugation established in the course of human history. As for Wollstonecraft, the emancipation of women implies a strategy of moving the centre of individual life from the private into the public sphere: 'The barriers must come down. One should educate citizens for the state, without any attention to sexual differences' (von Hippel, 1977: 133).

Fifth, however, von Hippel's argument also reveals a dilemma which the rationalist conception of emancipation by political change seems unable to resolve: the initiative can only come from men! Moral and historical arguments may unequivocally assert women's *entitlement* to full equality. Yet, there seems in practice no other way (since the idea of a feminist political movement was never considered in that time) than to appeal to the conscience and generosity of men – who, as von Hippel's analysis has clearly shown, have a vested interest in maintaining their superior power. The future of women, then, depends ultimately on the moral effects of enlightenment. They can only hope that their present oppressors will voluntarily abandon their privileges in favour of equality.

A revolution in female manners: 'by reforming themselves to reform the world'

In the dedication to the French minister Talleyrand which prefaces 'A Vindication of the Rights of Woman, (1975, originally published 1792), Mary Wollstonecraft throws the gauntlet to the legislators of revolutionary France who, despite their avowed belief in the 'natural rights of mankind', have excluded women (one half of the human race) from all participation in government. There is only one way, she maintains, of avoiding the charge of injustice and inconsistency: 'prove first . . . that they want reason' (Wollstonecraft, 1975: 88).

It is the aim of her book to ensure that such proof will never come forth. She rests her case on the following key assumptions: that reason – the capacity of acquiring knowledge, of forming judgements and of choosing general maxims of moral conduct – is of the *same kind* in women as in men; that reason is a necessary condition of virtue; that the emancipation of women towards equality demands the dominance of reason over the passions and – as regards their relationship with men – of rational fellowship over love.

The 'arrogant assumption of reason' according to which it is commonly appraised as a typically male capacity (1975: 206) lies at the root of all social and educational arrangements which have prevented women from attaining a sense of their own worth as rational and moral agents. It is this prejudice, the insistence 'to give a sex to mind' which prompts Wollstonecraft's most impassioned attacks on Rousseau.[3] She quotes at length (and with a clear sense that this alone will expose his absurd bias) those passages from *Emile* in which Rousseau infers from women's natural, physical weakness a limited capacity for knowledge bounded by practical concerns. They should, he had argued, not be encouraged to enquire into abstract and speculative truths nor to devote themselves to the study of science; 'as to the works of genius they are beyond their capacity' (an allegation which also drew a sarcastic comment from the romantic writer Friedrich Schlegel). Not men in general, but particular men – those whom they have to obey – should be the proper object of their study (quoted in Wollstonecraft, 1975: 125).

Against this extreme statement of the sexual character of our mental faculties Wollstonecraft sets her most fundamental belief that knowledge must be conceived as being the same in nature for both sexes and that excellence, whether of intellectual or moral pursuits, cannot be attained but by the same means. Knowledge, properly understood, consists in the 'power of generalising ideas, or drawing comprehensive conclusions from individual observations' (1975: 143). It demands, above all, disciplined and ordered procedures, exactness and perseverance in the search for truth. These qualities have so far been entirely lacking in the education of women who are in general only equipped for the 'random exertions of a sort of instinctive common sense never brought to the test of reason' (1975: 104). Genuine knowledge, furthermore, derives from the ability to form judgements by means of generalizing from matters of observation and not, as women have been taught to believe, from an 'individual manner of seeing things' (1975: 308, 311, 314).

Reason is identified with a single standard of systematic analytical thinking because only with such an orientation and training of the mind can we avoid becoming dependent on the opinions of others and submitting blindly to their authority. It is in virtue of being endowed with the *same* capacity of using our rational faculties as an instrument and guarantor of self-reliance that we can claim an equal right to freedom, that is, the right to judge our own happiness. Identity of reason must thus be seen as a necessary condition of equality of right. The same holds for the connection between reason and virtue. There can be no virtue born of innocence, no morality other than 'conscious virtue'. Innocence praised by so many modern writers on female education (most eloquently by Rousseau) as the natural moral disposition of the female sex is for Wollstonecraft but a 'specious name' for ignorance (1975: 100, 109). Due to the misconceived notion of natural sexual virtue unaided by knowledge, women have in the past been denied access to the opportunities to cultivate their understanding. And from the want of understanding have sprung 'all the causes that have degraded women' (1975: 172).

Because they thus derive the capacity for virtue as well as the entitlement to rights from autonomous reason and because autonomy is staked upon certain methods of acquiring knowledge, rationalists such as Wollstonecraft must insist on a single intellectual character in women and men. Unlike the romantic writers (and some feminists today), she will not admit that women might possess their own specifically feminine modes of understanding and might proceed towards the truth by different routes from men. Too much hinges on the sameness of reason: it is the only safeguard that human beings cannot be treated in a purely instrumental fashion by others (Wollstonecraft, 1975: 104, 144, 178; Lloyd, 1984: Chs. 4 and 5). To concede even the possibility of a differential or complementary nature of male and female reason – to suggest, for example, that the latter might be more directed by emotion and intuition than by systematic inquiry – would, from the perspective of her moral and political commitment, appear as the first step on a slippery slope towards that hierarchical ordering of different mental capabilities which has so often supplied the main pretext of women's submission.

Rousseau, again, proves the case in point: contrasting (in *Sophie* and *Emile*) a natural disposition for practical knowledge on the one hand, and for abstract reason on the other, he celebrates the wisdom of nature for having directed these sexual differences towards the perfect unity of man and woman as one moral being (Rousseau, *Emile*, in Wollstonecraft, 1975: 184). There is, however, no doubt that in this union one person's understanding and freedom is wholly dependent upon the superior judgement and will of the other and that what is conceived as female excellence is defined as such in relation to the ends of man. In the case of Rousseau, the sexual complementarity of intellectual character serves to justify the separate and inferior education of women which has but the one purpose of preparing them for life-long obedience to male authority.

It is, however, an open question whether it might not be possible to acknowledge specific, gender-based characteristics of reason without thereby implying the superiority or inferiority of one against the other. We shall see that the romantic notion of women's claim to independence contains the prerequisites for an affirmative answer.

Political and human emancipation

Given the assumptions about the essential identity of male and female nature, rationalist strategies for emancipation will aim to create the right conditions for women to prove their capacities as rational agents. In this they will give priority to the task of securing to women their rightful place in the public domain of civil society – as the equals and fellow citizens of men. Today this strategy is sometimes charged with an inadequate understanding of the causes of women's oppression. The preoccupation with formal equality of rights suffers, it is said, from the typical liberal illusion that women's present degradation is due chiefly to a defect in their legal position which might be corrected, as it were, by the stroke of constitutional amendments (see Jaggar, 1983: chs. 3 and 7; Schwarzer, 1983). Such criticism ignores those radical elements in the rationalist position which transcend the confines of a typical liberal viewpoint. The early advocates of women's rights are acutely aware of the forces that obstruct the emancipation of hitherto underprivileged groups. They realize that genuine equality for women cannot be achieved merely through the extension of legal entitlements because their capabilities have been cramped and their character warped through a long history of subjugation – to the point where they themselves have come to connive in their inferior position. This is why they place so much emphasis upon change through education. The schemes which they propose would have entailed a radical break with existing educational practices. They are designed to bring about a fundamental re-education of attitudes, a rooting out of the most deeply entrenched prejudices of modern society. Women will have to learn that their first duty is not towards men – in their roles as mothers, wives and daughters – but 'towards themselves as rational creatures' (Wollstonecraft, 1975: 257); men have to be brought to the point of accepting women as their companions rather than as domestic slaves or providers of pleasure.

To approach this goal, education must in all its manifold functions assume and reinforce the strict identity of intellectual and moral character in both sexes (Wollstonecraft, 1975: ch. 12, 'On National Education'; von Hippel, 1977: 130–146): for the greater part of their childhood boys and girls are to share the same educational environment. They must be instructed in the same subjects, enjoy the same games of leisure and – a point of particular importance to both von Hippel and Wollstonecraft – be subjected to the same physical exercises. The natural sexless sociability of children should be left to express itself in all their activities; equality is to reign even in their outward appearance (they should be dressed alike). Although later on some concessions have to be made to the acquisition of gender-specific skills geared to their respective professions and duties, these should never be allowed to disturb the basic uniformity of their future status as citizens.

But there are other reasons for doubting whether *political* enfranchisement and equal educational opportunities will suffice to ensure women's *human* emancipation. Just as Marx stressed the partial nature of political liberation because equality among citizens still leaves intact the relations of exploitation and domination in the economic sphere, feminists might say that the rationalist strategies ignore the root causes of women's oppression in the sexual division of labour within the family. However perceptive their analysis of this situation, none of the writers discussed in this chapter conceives of women's place other than as primarily in the home. Indeed, it appears that the development of their intellectual faculties and their inclusion in the rights of citizenship are geared to the very purpose of enabling them better to fulfil 'the peculiar duties of their sex': 'Make women rational creatures and free citizens, and they will quickly become good wives and mothers' (Wollstonecraft, 1975: 283, 299). Such concession to traditional roles does not fit easily into von Hippel's account which, as we have seen, identifies the division of labour in the family as the original evil and the cause of all further inequalities between the sexes. It is equally puzzling in the case of Wollstonecraft if we consider how strongly she endorses economic independence and access to hitherto exclusively male occupations as the condition of female freedom (1975: 150f., 182, 252, 261). Yet, the aspects of the new woman that receive most attention in the *Vindication* are those of a mother who actively and conscientiously discharges her domestic duties (that she should herself suckle her infants is repeatedly stressed as a major demand upon a female virtue) (1975: 140, 147f., 155ff., 252–63, 299).

However, when seen in the light of her radical political commitment and her passion for equality it is clear that the retained emphasis on domestic virtue does not spell capitulation to traditional values. The woman who herself takes an active interest in the upbringing of her children is set up in polemical contrast against the attitudes and corrupt practices prevailing in high society where mothers, for the sake of vanity, social reputation and frivolous pleasures, abandon their offspring to the care of domestic servants. Placed in its proper context Wollstonecraft's ideal of domestic virtue forms an integral part of her moral critique of civilized society corrupted by wealth and privilege (1975: 167, 254, 266). More importantly still, with regard to her vision of a future social order based upon equality of citizenship, one looks in vain for the private–public divide of the kind which preoccupies feminist political theory today.

The role which we commonly identify as belonging in the private sphere, Mary Wollstonecraft perceives as a constitutive element of citizenship. Stripped of their familiar association with intimate affections and merely personal interests, the tasks of a mother attain the dignity of public virtues. To the extent that women develop their understanding and become capable of comprehending and self-consciously performing their obligations, family life loses the character of secluded intimacy and becomes part of a domain of public concerns (1975: 314). Moreover, this transformation does not affect the position of women only. It reconstitutes the relations between them and men on an altogether new basis of rational fellowship.

This ideal illuminates yet another dimension in the problematic relationship and alleged divergence between political and human emancipation. It has been argued that in aspiring to be included in the 'Rights of Man', women have demanded for themselves what are, by origin and substance, the rights of men. In other words, the alleged universality of these rights is deceptive. In order to qualify as equal citizens, women must adopt values and attitudes and emulate standards of excellence that have been irrevocably shaped by the history of partriarchal domination (see Sichtermann, 1983: 103). This suspicion seems not unfounded. There is, indeed, evidence to suggest that the rationalist strategy for emancipation envisages a process whereby women must move towards a goal that men have already reached:

> They must enter upon the same path on which we had to exert ourselves; they must cross the same deserts which became so arduous to our journey towards Canaan; only through education, instruction and experience should they reach the destination of which they are so eminently worthy. (von Hippel, 1977: 132)

> Let women share the rights and they will emulate the virtues of men. (Wollstonecraft, 1975: 319)

Again, we can only answer the question posed here if we consider the nature and depth of political egalitarianism in this period. Behind the demand for equality – based upon the recognition in all human beings of an equal capacity for reason and virtue – stands the vision of a new age and of a regenerated society which extends far beyond changes merely in the state's legal and governmental organization. In the arguments of our writers the universalism postulated in the equal-rights principle combines two utopian expectations: that the demand for equality made by any underprivileged group includes the claims of all other such groups; and that equality of right will eventually change the very basis and quality of all human relationships within society. Thus the early feminist movements both in England and in America formed close links with the campaigns directed at the abolition of slavery (a connection confirmed by both Wollstonecraft (1975: 257) and von Hippel (1977: 61, 82f.) in frequent and illuminating analogies between the subjugation of women and the condition of slaves). In a different field, the title of von Hippel's book on the 'civil improvement of women' recalls the wording of one of the first German treatises (published in 1781) on behalf of Jewish emancipation: *On the Civil Improvement of the Jews* (Dohm, 1785). In considering the conditions of a possible future of mankind when 'the sun will shine only on free men who know no other master but their reason', Condorcet, in the *Sketch for a Historical Picture of the Progress of the Human Mind*, links equality between the sexes to the elimination of inequality between social classes as well as between nations (1976b pp. 258–81). That the oppression of women is both paradigmatic and part of an all-pervasive pattern of despotic power and social inequality is a recurrent theme in the *Vindication*. Conversely, the demand of equal rights does not mask a bid for power, but anticipates the end of all coercion in society: 'It is not empire, but equality that they should contend for' (Wollstonecraft, 1975: 204, 121f., 131f., 151, 285; see also Taylor, 1983: 5ff.). In this time, equality of civil and political right was still a promise to be cashed in by the majority of people. It was not an unreasonable hope that, if all groups so far excluded from citizenship were admitted, the very nature of civil society and of politics would change.

The second utopian dimension in the demand for political equality refers to the quality of personal relationships. It is hoped that, as a consequence of political emancipation, new bonds will emerge between individual human beings who have so far encountered each other only in positions of despotic power or helpless obedience – as masters and slaves, despots and subjects, husbands and wives. Equality will morally transform not only those who have been deprived of their rights but also those who have held rights only on the basis of might. What Paine said with regard to the abolition of aristocratic privilege applies also to the condition of men in relation to women: 'the *peer* is exalted into Man' (Paine, 1969: 102). Just as a society thus transformed would be altogether freed from the burden of social rank, so its members would in their relations to each other no longer need to submit to differences of sex.

In these two utopian dimensions political emancipation was (and could be) understood as human emancipation.

The link between the two could, however, be called into question if one were to assign a positive value to the special identity of individuals or groups, which should not be submerged in the general formula of a universal human right. This is the ground on which romanticism challenges the presuppositions of rationalist thinking. It repudiates the dictates of universal, uniform and immutable standards because they do not allow us to understand and appreciate what is particular, characteristic and of unique excellence in the provinces of beauty, morality and truth (see Lovejoy, 1960: ch. 10).

With regard to the emancipation of women the romantic opposition to the postulates of rationalism shall be construed along the following lines. First, the abstract ideal of the human person as a right-holder obliterates the particular gender-related individuality of women (as of men). It can claim universal validity only at the expense of suppressing the diversity in mental and emotional character traits. Secondly, the' primacy of reason, by virtue of which women are included in the rights of mankind, establishes a normative dualism, dividing the individual into separate warring factions, placing mind against body, rationality against sensuality. Thirdly, the ideal of 'rational fellowship' – thus constituted by uniformity of human nature and primacy of reason – must appear as a one-dimensional, impoverished form of relationship when compared to the liberating possibilities of mutual fulfilment that women and men can find in romantic love. Fourthly, what is at issue in the critique of women's oppression is not, in the first instance, a violation of moral principle, but an offence against the aesthetic ideal of femininity in which reason and feeling, desire for knowledge and the free expression of sensuality are brought into harmony. Fifthly, given these assumptions, neither the causes of women's subordination nor the conditions of their liberation will be sought in the domain of politics.

The romantic ideal of independent femininity
The defining characteristics of romantic thinking lie in the quest for individuality, diversity and organic wholeness. These principles were originally formulated in the field of literary and cultural criticism where they arose in rebellion to the rigid standards of perfection that neo-classicism imposed upon the practice and critical appreciation of art. Against the demands for order, symmetry and uniformity in the artistic representation of life, the romantics emphasize spontaneity, originality and infinite variety of authentic self-expression. For the same reason that they reject uniform standards of excellence in art, they distrust all universal formulas in morality and politics. Any rules which invoke the authority of immutable nature or timeless reason are seen as impositions on the freedom of individual self-realization. With regard to the romantic understanding of human nature, individuality of character is not a given datum. It evolves in a continuous open-ended process of self-education (*Bildung*) typically

conceived in analogy with the freedom of artistic creation. The romantic writers rebel against the prevailing sexual stereotype of 'pure femininity' which casts the female character into a narrow frame of domesticity, 'false modesty' and dependence on men, because it does not allow for the extensive and unconstrained development in each woman of her individual potential:

> Their own sense of purpose, their own energy and will are what is most human, most original, most sacred in human beings. Whether they belong to this or that sex is by comparison, insignificant and contingent. (Schlegel, 1983: 91)

It is, furthermore, in the nature of general norms which lay claim to absolute validity that they will elevate one single form of the good or the beautiful at the expense of excluding all others. If one lays down standards of perfection exclusively by reference to the classical Greek temple one will never be able to perceive in the Gothic style anything but an aberration from the ideal, a manifestation of sheer disorder and ugliness (see Wellek, 1981: 57ff.; Eitner, 1970: 21). Similarly, if one reduces the search for truth to a single mode and method of rational enquiry one might well accept the absurd belief that women lack by nature a disposition and talent for philosophy. In fact, such a belief reflects only the narrow-mindedness of people incapable of understanding that women have their own and equally valuable ways of approaching philosophical questions (see Schlegel, 1983: 66, 86). Romantic thinking wants to apprehend the intrinsic value in all, and be it the most diverse, manifestations of human nature. Because it delights in those qualities in which individual persons (as well as works of art, languages and whole cultures) are unlike each other, it considers the diversity of male and female dispositions as a stimulus and a source of energy which can encourage the development of a rich and many-faceted character. This sensitivity to qualitative differences and the endeavour to embrace the plenitude of possible experience is complemented by an equally strong desire for integration. Romanticism experiments with artistic styles and forms of human relationships in which diversity can be brought into harmony without destroying or curbing individuality. Love between women and men constitutes the paradigm for this principle of integration – for a power capable of creating a unity in which individuation and diversity survive without division (see Abrams, 1971: 292–9).

Reflection on the nature of femininity commands a place of strategic importance in the romantic writers' rebellion against the dominant values of their time. It is intimately related to the critical intention of their philosophical and poetic theories which seek to overcome the crisis of the modern age in new developments of art as well as new forms of sociability. In his earliest studies of classical Greek literature and philosophy, Friedrich Schlegel shows how a 'theory of Greek femininity' would enable us to gain a deeper understanding of ancient culture and, by contrast, of modern civilization.[4] His friend, Schleiermacher, speaks in a similar vein of the decisive impulse and direction that the study of women has given to all his philosophical pursuits: 'I could only live and thrive in an age where one has begun to understand women' (quoted in Kluckhohn, 1931: 432).

'Exaggerated femininity' – a critique of modern prejudice
In the fusion of seemingly contradictory elements – universalist autonomy and gender-determined character – the romantic ideal of self-reliant femininity stands apart both from the traditionalist claim of women's natural incapacity for freedom and from the rationalist postulate of sexless humanity. In Friedrich Schlegel's earliest writings this ideal denotes, indeed celebrates, the deviations from the accepted norms of female propriety (1983: 55). In the Diotima of Plato's *Symposium*, in the female pupils of the Pythagorean school of philosophy and in Sparta's women who took part in masculine exercises and were, as mothers, willing to sacrifice the most 'natural' feelings to the demands of patriotism, he discovers a lost history of independent womanhood. He is aware that to the guardians of contemporary morality these 'masculine' pursuits of Greek women must appear as the destruction of femininity itself, just as Sappho's genius will never be honoured among those philistine censors of taste who, like Rousseau, believe that women are by nature incapable of poetic enthusiasm and artistic creativity (1983: 59–65). In thus confronting modern stereotypes with provocative images of female independence, Schlegel stresses the ideological distortions and the epistemological confusion in the modern perception of woman's nature. Why are the moderns so loath to recognize in those examples from the past a superior, more developed form of womanhood? The answer must be because they have exaggerated the natural differences between the sexes into a rigid scheme of mutually exclusive qualities. They find it difficult even to imagine that there was a time when (in Sparta) 'women possessed masculine strength and independence while young men displayed female modesty, shame and gentleness' (1983: 59). What to them seems but a perversion of nature's imperatives is, in fact, proof of the human capacity for freedom – freedom of individuals to move beyond the separate prescriptions of male and female virtue towards a common ideal of *Menschlichkeit*. That these sexual stereotypes, each made up of an extensive

catalogue of exclusively male and female characteristics, have assumed the status of self-evident truths reflects the self-interest and power of men: the ideal of pure femininity, with its emphasis on innocence and helplessness, serves as a convenient rationalization of the desire that women should exist *for* men. Their self-interest is reinforced by confusion – most people fail to distinguish the essential, constitutive features in the idea of a human person from its merely contingent associations. This is why they crowd into the notion of femininity numerous attributes derived from particular circumstances of time and place. Thus the unashamed expression of sensual passion that can be found among women in southern climates will be condemned as an aberration from the natural dictates of female chastity although the latter are in fact but a reflection of 'northern frostiness' elevated into a universal trait of human nature (1983: 72).

This is the salient point in Schlegel's account of Greek femininity: it challenges any belief in an immutable sexual nature. Such a tribute to the determining power of nature would, he claims, be incompatible with the striving for freedom and beauty. The selfless unbounded devotion of a wife – extolled by many modern writers as the most admirable among female virtues – is but a shameful renunciation of independence betraying 'absolute lack of character':

> Both, the impatient will to dominate in man and the self-denying submissiveness in woman are exaggerated and ugly. Only self-reliant womanhood and gentle manhood deserve to be called good and beautiful. (Schlegel, 1983: 61)

The specific merit and emancipatory tendency of Schlegel's earliest reflections on the defining characteristics of women and men does not lie in an alternative account of human nature. He does not match prevailing beliefs about women by equally authoritative counter-assertions. His critique is, on the contrary, directed against the very assumption of a nature exhaustively defined by certain invariable attributes. The intention is to leave the conception of woman's (and man's) nature as empty and open-ended as possible. Natural differences are conceived as a kind of raw material out of which individuals are free to create their own character. Unlike von Hippel, however, Schlegel does not relegate sexual identity and difference to insignificant, merely contingent attributes. The notions of femininity and masculinity have not become redundant. The aim is 'to subordinate – without destroying it – gender-being to species-being' (1983: 60).

Statements such as this betray some ambiguity as to how we should conceive of the relationship between gender, as a natural disposition, and individual character, as the product of freedom. Is the former 'a mere appendage to human existence' (Schlegel, 1983: 91)? Or is its influence upon the individual so decisive that, in Schleiermacher's words, 'it would be absurd to ignore the sexual identity of the soul' (quoted in Kluckhohn, 1931: 462)? In one instance, Schlegel refers to gender as a 'stimulus of nature' (*Ermunterung der Natur*) (1983: 60, 92ff.). It imparts to the female person the distinct qualities of *motherliness* (*Mütterlichkeit*) and *sympathy*. Although the former is said to be an original and essential attribute of female nature, it clearly does not refer to a simple biological fact. It forms the basis of (and is reflected in) the disposition for sympathy – for a woman's capacity to harmonize experience and knowledge from an inner centre of intuitive understanding and reflective feeling.

Female reason
This capacity Schlegel considers as the distinct feature of female reason. Here, then, we encounter an assumption of differential rationality which, as has been shown, is rejected by the rationalist as incompatible with the idea of women's autonomy. We have to bear in mind, however, that in the romantic context this assumption is asserted *against* the orthodox belief that women lack the capacity for philosophical knowledge. We are not dealing here with what is often referred to as a typically 'romantic' view – of women as 'wordless, mindless nature' (Jaggar, 1983: 115). On the contrary, their emergence from the restrictive circle of domestic concerns and from the bond of submissiveness is predicated upon the sincere and systematic pursuit of knowledge. Moreover, female reason is in many respects regarded as superior, rather than inferior, to the modes of reasoning in which men excel (Schlegel, 1983: 66; Schleiermacher, 1964: 104ff.). Although women are perhaps less equipped for the rigour of analytical thinking and abstract speculation, their 'lyrical philosophizing' will in many cases, where men's rationality tends towards dissection, isolation and fragmentation, come closer to embracing the whole and undivided nature of truth. The well-worn comparison between analytical and intuitive modes of knowledge turns in romantic thinking often to the disadvantage of the former: enslaved to abstraction and lacking in feeling and imagination, men's reason is prone to neglect the wholeness of experience.

If the rationalist belief in the simple uniformity of reason is thus denied, it is equally true that, for the romantics, gender-related differences in emotional and cognitive faculties do not convey connotations of superiority and inferiority. More importantly still, they do not constitute *absolute* divides. The complementarity of gender characteristics is stated in a general context in which women still have to develop their potential and men's present 'nature' is not taken for granted. The latter is more radically questioned than in rationalist thinking which, in many respects, conceives of women's emanci-

pation as a movement towards already established models of excellence.
present 'nature' taken for granted. The latter is more radically
questioned than in rationalist thinking which, in many respects,
conceives of women's emancipation as a movement towards already
established models of excellence.

Female rationality, furthermore, can – without incurring the usual
suspicion of lesser competence – be associated with emotive qualities
because the romantic ideal of self-realization demands the cultivation
and exercise of all human faculties: of feeling, desire, and passion no
less than of rational understanding. Whereas Mary Wollstonecraft's
case for women's equality depends crucially upon defending the
primacy of reason against the intrusion of 'tumultuous passion'
(Wollstonecraft, 1975: 110), the romantic idea of female independence
includes the liberation of female sexuality. Indeed, the
suppression of woman's desire and capacity for sexual fulfilment in
the prescriptions of chastity and 'false modesty' ('Englanderism' in
the romantic terminology) is seen as the most powerful agent of her
oppression (see Schlegel, 1983: 72; Schleiermacher, 1964: 104f.).
Wollstonecraft's understanding of domestic virtue betrays a
profound distrust of sensuality, as if it were indistinguishable from
the dark shadows of vice. Her abhorrence and severe condemnation
of adultery and prostitution (and her rather priggish attitude towards
the naked body) contrast strongly with the unprudish appraisal of
sensuous beauty and genuine passion that can be found in the
romantic literature of Schlegel's generation. He himself wrote a
novel that tells the story of a love relationship unconstrained by
artificial rules of propriety, which fortifies and develops all human
desires (see Dischner, 1980). It caused an enormous scandal in its
time and was proscribed as obscene until well into the twentieth
century. What shocked the reading public was, above all, the
suggestion that a woman should, like a man, be able and be permitted
to feel sexual passion.

Emancipation through love

In terms of most distinctions between the private and public sphere,
love would seem to stand in polar opposition to, and in clear
separation from, politics. Love is not a political issue; it belongs in the
sanctuary of intimate personal behaviour; political relationships have
an altogether different quality from bonds of love. However, in the
arguments which we are going to consider here love occupies, or
usurps, a space in which the meaningfulness of these distinctions
becomes blurred.

Love plays a pivotal role in both romantic and rationalist conceptions
of women's emancipation. While in the former it is celebrated
as an agent of liberation, due to its unique power to free individuals

from the fetters of repressive conventions, it emerges from the latter as a major threat to woman's independence – as a beautiful facade which embellishes and conceals the reality of her degradation. For the defenders of women's equal rights, love poses an intractable problem. 'Rational fellowship' which guarantees this equality depends upon the undisturbed dominance of reason. Since love constitutes a form of human relationship which, more than any other, thrives upon and magnifies the differences between men and women, and since it elevates feeling above reason, they are by the logic of their position compelled to relegate it to a place of secondary importance. It is thus altogether omitted from the reasons and observations from which Condorcet and von Hippel infer the basic sameness of male and female nature. In Mary Wollstonecraft we find passages of deep ambiguity, of tortured and anguished reasoning which seeks to contain the damage that passionate love might wreak upon a woman's path towards independence. It is true, her main concern is to demask and combat those illusions which in overwhelming the mind with 'false dreams of happiness'[5] have made woman the willing accomplice in her own subjugation. However, the bitterness felt at the state of dependence – of feigned weakness ('sickly delicacy') and overheated sensibility – into which women have been lured by the 'fallacious light of sentiment' (Wollstonecraft, 1975: 134), seems to drive Wollstonecraft into an all-out war against the passion of love itself where she is no longer willing to distinguish the genuine sentiment from its impostors. Under the spell of emotions infused with the power of sensuality, virtue – so it seems – will of necessity succumb to 'mere appetite', with 'chance and sensation' taking the place of 'choice and reason' (1975: 113). By contrast, in the virtuous marriage the fever of passion has abated and given way to the 'healthy temperature' of well regulated affections ('in order to fulfil the duties of life . . . a master and mistress of a family ought not to continue to love each other with passion') (1975: 113f.). Love between husband and wife expresses itself in mutual respect, in paternal affections and maternal solicitude. The power of sexual desire has been successfully curbed – albeit at the price of an austere and, romantically speaking, rather dull regime.

It is again important at this point to stress the political dimension in Wollstonecraft's quest for women's freedom. The primary aim of the 'revolution in female manners' is not personal happiness – understood as gratification of hitherto proscribed desires – but rather the subordination of such desires to self-conscious, republican virtue. In this sense, the personal relationships of marriage must assume a public character. Conversely, she fears in love a destructive power extending well beyond the boundaries of the merely private sphere.

To the extent that the passions engross thoughts and energies that should be deployed for higher purposes and thus distract individuals from the 'employments that form the moral character' (Wollstone-craft, 1975: 114f.), they threaten to disturb the order of society. It is on this premise of wanting to transform the private into a public person that friendship, as 'the most holy bond of society' (1975: 113ff.), is given priority over love:

> Friendship is a serious affection; the most sublime of all affections, because it is founded on principle, and cemented by time. The very reverse may be said of love. (1975: 167)

Contrary to what 'romantic love' has come to mean in common language – unbounded feeling overwhelming sound reason and posing a threat to rational self-control – in early romantic theory it is credited with a power that encourages the discovery of the self. To love is to inspire another person's development; each releases in the other energies that will bring them closer towards what they might achieve as human beings. Since freedom is understood as a process of self-creation in which all individual faculties and endeavours are activated, and since the polarity of female and male nature can act as a stimulus upon such development, love constitutes the proper sphere of emancipation. It creates a space outside the relations of domination and submission which society has imposed upon individuals.

Romantic love allows for the uninhibited, ecstatic expression of all passions 'from the most exuberant sensuality to the most spiritual spirituality' (Schlegel, 1964: 10). It does not ignore nor discard the different sexual identities of women and men but it continually shifts their boundaries. This, I think, is the most important idea that romantic thinking has contributed to the debate on women's emanci-pation. It postulates in the openness of human nature the space for excursions into foreign territory – for the possibility that individuals will discover and cultivate in themselves dispositions commonly ascribed to the other sex. What is possible on the basis of female and male nature cannot be inferred from the conventional division of sexual roles; it is something with which women and men have the freedom to play and experiment. The freedom to be gained in playfully transcending the apparent limits of natural sexual roles is praised in a famous passage in Schlegel's novel *Lucinde* – the 'Dithyrambic Phantasy about the most Delightful Situation' (a passage which much scandalized the contemporary reading public). It describes the delight that lovers can experience in swapping masculine and feminine roles in sexual intercourse:

> Among all situations I consider this the funniest and most beautiful: when we exchange roles and compete in childish delight who of us is better in imitating the other – whether you are more successful in pretending to the cautious impetuosity of a man, or I in feigning the attractive passivity of a woman. (1964: 12)

That this was not a scandalous account of perverse practices but, in its unashamed tribute to sensual passion, at the same time an allegory intimating 'the perfection of masculinity and femininity towards full and complete humanity' escaped most of Schlegel's readers.

The utopia of free sociability

While in the rationalist vision the emancipation of women depends upon a transformation in the political relationships among individuals, the romantic ideal of self-reliant femininity refers to a process of liberation that takes place outside the public sphere. Through love, friendship and intellectual companionship woman will become the equal of man, but the political conditions of her subordination remain unchanged. Although in bed sexual roles are reversed and society's conventions toppled, woman's traditional place inside the home is taken for granted; so is her inferior legal status. It is a dominant theme in romantic thinking that in society as it presently exists individual freedom can be realized only in opposition to, and in seclusion from, the world of politics (a world of prejudice, vulgar taste and aimless activity). What good would it do, asks Schlegel, to become a mere number in the great political sum (1983: 99)? It is a woman's privilege that she need not get involved in the petty affairs of public life which a man, however reluctantly in the case of the romantic poet, will always have to confront (1983: 96).

However, to confine the romantic idea of independent womanhood to a secluded sphere of private happiness hermetically sealed off from society at large would be to ignore – here, too – a utopian, subversive tendency that aims at transforming the very basis of civil society. It is true, the romantics do not expect such change to come about through political participation. Rather, they envisage a process that will radiate outwards from the centres of private life. They entrust love and friendship with the power of creating alternative forms of sociability, based upon free association, spontaneity, mutual affections unconstrained by social etiquette and formal legal arrangements. In this sense, they see themselves as 'citizens of a new world' built upon the intimacy of liberated personal relations, on the one hand, and a sense of universal 'brotherhood' on the other:

> . . . instead of an artificial society, there should only be marriage between the two estates of women and men, and a universal brotherhood of all individuals. (Schlegel, 1964: 70)

Conclusion

I have tried to show in this chapter that in the eighteenth century the case for women's emancipation could be made on very different and, in many respects, incompatible assumptions – of a universalist, genderless human nature, on the one hand, and of a distinctly feminine character, on the other. It is tempting to interpret these ideas in the light of subsequent political and ideological developments.[6] Thus, as they move from the ideas of Mary Wollstonecraft to those of J.S. Mill and the Suffragists, and then further into the twentieth century, critics of liberal feminism have identified its major weakness with an unresolved tension between the commitment to women's formal equality in the public sphere and an uncritical acquiescence in the inequalities of power within the family. Too much trust was placed in changes that would follow upon the admission of women to legal and political rights on the same conditions as men. Preoccupied with the struggle for the vote and with the assertion of rights on behalf of middle-class women, liberal advocates of sexual equality underestimated the material forces – in the market as well as in the family – which militated against genuine independence and full participation for the majority of women.

Similarly, one might detect in the romantic ideal of love that tendency towards a sentimentalization and privatization of values which – through a retreat from, and denigration of, the world of politics – became one of the most potent ideological devices to disguise and perpetuate the reality of male power and female subjugation. Moreover, to claim an intrinsic superiority for specifically feminine moral and intellectual attributes could be seen to reinforce, albeit unwittingly, the very reasons by virtue of which women had always been confined to the pursuits of a separate and secluded sphere. (Thus, for example, the anti-suffragists in a later period would contend that for women to enter public life must invariably lead to the corruption of their superior moral character.)

Because they did not break decisively with those assumptions which defined the position of women by a particular, 'natural' closeness to the sphere of reproduction and domestic labour, the early feminist writers under discussion here did not, in the end, bring about the conceptual revolution necessary for the development of feminist political theory. Judged from the vantage point of today they remained prisoners of the dominant paradigm of politics which rests on an arbitrary split between what is political and what is not, and which has continued to mystify the real roots of women's oppression.

Although it need not be denied that rationalist and romantic arguments could be, and were, used in this manner I would claim that in their original historical context they were genuinely emancipatory.

In the ideals of rational fellowship and of romantic love they contained utopian elements which associated women's liberation with fundamental changes in human relationships and, as a consequence, in the very nature of political society.

Notes

1. In this chapter the term 'rationalism' is used only to refer to emancipatory views on women's nature and their place in civil society. Rationalist assumptions, however, did in the eighteenth century also serve as the basis of a conservative position which stated the essential inequality between the sexes as founded in reason and nature. For the ambivalence of Enlightenment rationalism in this respect, see Kluckhohn (1931: chs. 1–5).

2. For the philosophical and aesthetic doctrine of early German romanticism, see Lovejoy (1948a and 1948b), and Wellek (1981: chs. 1–3). In this chapter I shall concentrate upon the writings of Schlegel (1983 and 1964) and Schleiermacher (1964).

3. See Wollstonecraft (1975: chs. 2, 3 and 5). Wollstonecraft's attitude towards Rousseau is deeply divided between admiration and antagonism. Like many radicals of her time, she owes to Rousseau the perception of the vices and corruption of modern society. From Rousseau, too, derives the passion for equality and virtue which is the dominant impulse in her argument: her aim is to *extend* to women what Rousseau has asserted with regard to men (1975: 103).

4. See the essays, 'Über die weiblichen Charaktere in den griechischen Dichtern' (1794); and 'Über die Diotima' (1795), in Schlegel (1983: 11–38, 39–84).

5. Wollstonecraft (1975: 116). She expresses the hope that love will 'acquire more serious dignity' once women have developed reasoning so as to match feeling – 'the only province of woman at present' (1975: 223). See also Walters (1976: 305f.).

6. For the main points raised in this concluding section, see Eisenstein (1981), Elshtain (1982), Krouse (1982), Mitchell (1976), Morgan (1975), Okin (1982), Rover (1967) and Harrison (1978).

References

Abrams, M.H. (1971) *Natural Supernaturalism. Tradition and Revolution in Romantic Literature*. New York: W.W. Norton.

Baker, K.M. (1976) 'Introduction' to Condorcet, *Selected Writings*, K.M. Baker (ed.). Indianapolis: Bobbs-Merrill.

Condorcet A., Marquis de, (1976a) 'On the Admission of Women to the Rights of Citizenship', pp. 97–104 in Condorcet, *Selected Writings*, K.M. Baker (ed.). Indianapolis: Bobbs-Merrill (first published 1790).

Condorcet A., Marquis de, (1976b) 'Sketch for a Historical Picture of the Progress of the Human Mind', pp. 258–81 in Condorcet, *Selected Writings*, K.M. Baker (ed.). Indianapolis: Bobbs-Merrill (first published 1795).

Dischner, G. (1980) *Friedrich Schlegel's Lucinde und Materialien zu einer Theorie des Müssiggangs*. Hildesheim: Gerstenberg Verlag.

Dohm, C.W. (1781) *Über die bürgerliche Verbesserung der Juden*. Berlin.

Eisenstein, Z. (1981) *The Radical Future of Liberal Feminism*. New York: Longman.

Eitner, L. (1970) *Neoclassicism and Romanticism 1750–1850*. Vol. II. Englewood Cliffs, NJ: Prentice Hall.

Elshtain, J. Bethke (1982) 'Aristotle, the Public–Private Split, and the Case of the Suffragists', pp. 57–65 in J. Bethke Elshtain (ed.), *The Family in Political Thought*. Brighton: Harvester.

Graham, R. (1977) 'Loaves and Liberty: Women in the French Revolution', pp. 236–54 in R. Bridenthal and C. Koonz (eds.), *Becoming Visible. Women in European History*. Boston: Houghton Mifflin.

Green, J.P. (1976) *All Men are Created Equal*. Oxford: Clarendon Press.

Harrison, B. (1978) *Separate Spheres. The Opposition to Women's Suffrage in Britain*. London: Croom Helm.

Jaggar, A.M. (1983) *Feminist Politics and Human Nature*. Brighton: Harvester.

Kluckhohn, P. (1931) *Die Auffassung der Liebe in der Literatur des 18. Jahrhunderts und in der deutschen Romantik*, 2nd ed. Halle: Max Niemeyer Verlag.

Krouse, R.W. (1982) 'Patriarchal Liberalism and Beyond: From John Stuart Mill to Harriet Taylor', pp. 145–72 in J. Bethke Elshtain (ed.), *The Family in Political Thought*. Brighton: Harvester.

Lloyd, G. (1984) *The Man of Reason. 'Male' and 'Female' in Western Philosophy*. London: Methuen.

Lovejoy, A. (1948a) 'The Meaning of "Romantic" in Early German Romanticism', pp. 183–206 in A. Lovejoy, *Essays in the History of Ideas*. Baltimore and London: Johns Hopkins University Press.

Lovejoy, A. (1948b) 'Schiller and the Genesis of German Romanticism', pp. 207–27 in A. Lovejoy, *Essays in the History of Ideas*. Baltimore and London: Johns Hopkins University Press.

Lovejoy, A.O. (1960) *The Great Chain of Being. A Study of the History of an Idea*. New York: Harper & Row.

Mitchell, J. (1976) 'Women and Equality', pp. 379–99 in A. Oakley and J. Mitchell (eds), *The Rights and Wrongs of Women*. Harmondsworth: Penguin.

Morgan, D. (1975) *Suffragists and Liberals. The Politics of Woman Suffrage in England*. Oxford: Blackwell.

Okin, S. Moller (1982) 'Women and the Making of the Sentimental Family', *Philosophy and Public Affairs*, 11(1): 65–88.

Paine, Thomas (1969) *Rights of Man*. Harmondsworth: Penguin (first published 1791/92).

Rover, C. (1967) *Women's Suffrage and Party Politics in Britain 1866–1914*. London: Routledge.

Schlegel, Friedrich (1983) *Theorie der Weiblichkeit*, W. Menninghaus (ed.). Frankfurt: Insel Verlag.

Schlegel, Friedrich (1964) Lucinde. Frankfurt: Insel Verlag (first published 1799).

Schleiermacher, Friedrich (1964) *Vertraute Briefe Uber Friedrich Schlegel's Lucinde*. Frankfurt: Insel Verlag (first published 1800).

Schwarzer, A. (1983) *So fing es an! Die neue Frauenbewegung*. Munich: Deutscher Taschenbuch Verlag.

Sichtermann, B. (1983) *Weiblichkeit. Zur Politik des Privaten*. Berlin: Wagenbach.

Taylor, B. (1983) *Eve and the New Jerusalem. Socialism and Feminism in the Nineteenth Century*. London: Virago.

von Hippel, Theodor (1977) *Über die Bürgerliche Verbesserung der Weiber*. Frankfurt: Syndicat (first published 1793).

Walters, M. (1976). 'The Rights and Wrongs of Women', in A. Oakley and J. Mitchell (eds), *The Rights and Wrongs of Women*. Harmondsworth: Penguin.

Wellek, R. (1981) *A History of Modern Criticism 1750–1950. 2. The Romantic Age*. Cambridge: Cambridge University Press.

Wollstonecraft, M. (1975) *A Vindication of the Rights of Woman*. Harmondsworth: Penguin (first published 1792).

3
Crossing the river of fire: the socialist construction of women's politicization

Karen Hunt

Preface

To build a feminist political theory it is important to analyse how theories and ideologies have constructed our understanding of society. It is only on this basis that society can be changed. Ideas always have a context and a complex history, for individual thinkers and ideologies are a product, in some way or another, of the society of which they are a part. Feminism itself has evolved over generations although, as with other ideologies, this has not always been in an even or unilinear fashion. But that development has been within particular parameters, in this case those of patriarchy, as well as in response to other competing explanations of power in society such as liberalism, socialism and Marxism. As feminists we need to reclaim our history and understand the complex construction of what we now know as feminism. It is also necessary to analyse those ideologies which have shaped our thinking and structured our experience of gender and our explanations of women's oppression. It seems to me that all of this is part of the project of building a feminist political theory.

Such a vast undertaking of deconstructing and then reconstructing a gendered societal analysis is not merely a theoretical exercise. Theory only really has meaning provided it has a mutually informing relationship with practice. Only by tracing back the complex conceptual and historical roots of socialism, for example, can we begin to examine the way that a particular ideology has constructed women's experience. This process is therefore more than an elaboration of the concepts and arguments concerned, as would be adopted in a pure 'history of ideas' approach. It also involves taking such concepts beyond the abstract to an examination of their development within a historical context.

The process of deconstruction is clearly distinguished from one of demolition for it is not necessary to reject per se every aspect of an ideology or theory because of its overall inadequacies in relation to gender. But the recognition of these inadequacies must colour our perceptions of the ideology or theory as a whole. The process of deconstruction means bringing a different set of questions to bear in any analysis as well as being aware that the explicit content of a theory is not necessarily the sole determinant of its meaning.

47

Ambiguities and absences are just as influential. The assumptions on which any theory rests have to be explored to examine the way in which women's experience is conceptualized either explicitly or by its absence, for this in turn affects the theory as practised.

One key ideology that feminists are concerned to re-evaluate is socialism. Socialism and feminism have affected one another's evolution, in both a pro-active and a re-active manner, and many of the roots of their conceptual development are tangled together. More specifically those of us who are socialists and feminists are trying to establish a more analytically persuasive means of cementing the two analyses – one of class society and the other of patriarchy – with more than just a hyphen, as in 'socialist-feminism' (see, for example, Eisenstein, ed., 1979; Sargent, ed., 1981). As part of this project it is important to examine how socialism and socialists have constructed what in the nineteenth century came to be called the Woman Question. This term covers the breadth of issues which are part of any explanation of women's position in society and how it can be alleviated. Its content therefore includes all aspects of the relations between the sexes in the public sphere, including work and politics, and also in the private sphere, including the family, marriage and sexuality. It must also entail the ways in which the notions of the public and the private themselves are conceptualized. The Woman Question was, indeed, a shorthand for all these issues and specifically dealt with the question of women's oppression.

In this chapter I look at a particular aspect of socialism and the Woman Question by looking at the way in which women's politicization was conceptualized and how this therefore affected women's perception of socialism. This leads me to the image in the chapter title and the broader question of how socialists, and specifically women socialists, come to be made. William Morris used the powerful image of a 'river of fire' to describe the significant transition between being a non-socialist and being a socialist. He wrote that:

> between us and that which is to be . . . there is something alive and devouring; something as it were a river of fire that will put all that tries to swim across to a hard proof indeed, and scare from the plunge every soul that is not made fearless by desire of truth and insight of the happy days to come beyond. (quoted in Thompson, 1977: 244)

When Morris was writing in the 1880s, becoming a socialist had wide social costs including victimization, which explains some of the force of this image. But its description of the personal and the more general significance of becoming a socialist still has resonances for us today. Morris's image is also suggestive of the daunting task that awaits those socialists who attempt to persuade others to cross the 'river of fire'. Yet it was, and is, precisely that task of 'making socialists', as Morris called it, that is necessary if socialism is to be achieved. But within socialist theory and practice there is remarkably little guidance on the journey across that river. It is this process of becoming which is the focus of this chapter. How are socialists made and, more specifically, how do women become socialists? Is the socialist model of politicization gender-specific, either by design or by default? What are the ramifications of this for socialists in general and women in particular?

A context for this discussion is provided by concentrating on historical material which highlights the way in which women have been perceived theoretically and practically by a socialist organization. The Social Democratic Federation (SDF) was Britain's first Marxist party and covers the period from 1884 through and into the First World War, although it did continue as a shadow of itself beyond this period. The pre-First World War period is of interest because it witnessed a major confrontation between socialism and feminism, and hence saw the framework being set for the socialists' understanding of the Woman Question. This formulation has remained largely unchallenged until quite recently. In many ways the ambiguities and concerns of that earlier period still shape socialism's perception of women. It is these resonances which provide the key to the relevance of the material. The need to ask the questions should, I hope, be obvious.

The theory

The SDF's understanding of socialism was essentially an orthodox Marxist one. That is, for them the crucial divide in society was economic and everything else was secondary. This led to a fairly narrow definition of issues which were crucial to socialist politics, in contrast to a wide variety of others, such as religion, teetotalism and feminism, which were defined as peripheral. So as the SDF's columnist, the Tattler, emphasized:

> I think it should be always made clear that Socialism deals only with the economic question and however much any of us may speculate on the changes in sexual relations that may result from changed economic conditions, the individual making them is responsible for such speculations, and they are to be in nowise regarded as part of socialist teaching. (*Justice*, 21 September 1895)

Anything beyond the strictly economic was a matter for the individual conscience and as such could not be used to impugn anyone's socialist credentials. Thus, for example, Belfort Bax[1] was able not only to have his misogynist views printed in *Justice*, the SDF's newspaper, despite opposition from women and men, but also to have his right to do so defended editorially. This defence consisted of the terms outlined by the Tattler above, coupled with a broader appeal to the right to freedom of speech. So although this policy alienated potential women members, this was seen as merely a side effect (unfortunate or otherwise) of a sound political principle.

Given that these matters were characterized by an absence of consensus, it was therefore thought better not to give time to the 'conscience' issues as they only diverted energies from the current economic question. So:

> it is the economic conditions we have to attack and . . . when these have been changed these abstract questions will settle themselves. (*Justice*, 28 December 1895)

Any discussion of the Woman Question ensured that these arguments swung into action, for example, prompting correspondence under the heading of 'The Cult of Abstractions'. The danger was thought to be clear:

> My only objection to the so-called 'Woman Question' was that it threatened a division in our ranks by directing the attention of women from the real enemy, capitalism, to an imaginary enemy, an abstract 'brute man'. (*Justice*, 16 May 1896)

Therefore the limited definition of socialism itself dovetailed neatly with a pragmatic concern to marginalize such 'conscience' issues as the Woman Question. Any 'cult' of these 'abstractions' would promote internal disagreement and consequently, so it was argued, would divert energy from socialism itself. The solution was therefore a limited but specific manifesto of public economic objectives coupled with the democratic right to pursue one's own conscience over private matters. Maximum unity and solidarity could then be maintained around this formulation, hence the continued appeal of the 'broad church' approach to the British labour movement. What is of concern here is how this affects the socialist construction of the Woman Question, and therefore women's perception of socialism.

These general arguments around a range of 'conscience' issues together underlined the primacy of the economic to socialists. But they were more specifically reinforced in the case of feminism by the approach taken by socialists to the Woman Question in particular. The socialist understanding of the Woman Question rested on Engels's *The Origin of the Family, Private Property and the State*, first published in 1884, and most specifically on August Bebel's *Woman under Socialism*, first published in 1879. Both Engels and Bebel argued that the Woman Question could only be resolved under a socialist society and that, therefore, it was in women's interests to join with the proletariat in the fight to overthrow capitalism. Bebel argued:

> the Woman Question is only one of the aspects of the Social Question, which is now filling all heads, which is setting all minds in motion and which, consequently, can find its final solution only in the abolition of the existing social contradictions and of the evils which flow from them. (Bebel, 1971: 1)

Although this formulation in fact provided fuel for very different practical interpretations of the relevance of the Woman Question to socialists, these two key works did not spawn other significant contributions to the debate. The eminence of the authors, as founding fathers of socialism, served to make these the last rather than only the first words on the subject, for this and subsequent generations of socialists. This in turn gave even greater significance to the ambiguities, absences and limitations of these two texts.

Of the two works, Bebel's was the more widely read. After publication in 1879, it went through twenty-five editions by 1895 and reached its fiftieth German edition in 1910. In the years before 1914 *Woman under Socialism* was the most popular book borrowed from workers' libraries in Germany (see Steinberg, 1976). But it also had considerable significance beyond the German Social Democratic Party (SPD), to the Second International as a whole. It was translated widely and the first English language edition appeared in 1885. It was far more widely advertised and directly referred to within *Justice* than Engel's work, although there is evidence that *The Origin of the Family, Private Property and the State* was also being read by socialist activists (see, for example, McShane and Smith, 1978).[2]

Bebel's book, *Woman under Socialism*, paradoxically had the effect of marginalizing women within contemporary socialist concerns while also drawing women more firmly into the socialist arena. It inspired many women into undertaking, or continuing, the journey across the 'river of fire'. One example to illustrate this is Ottilie Baader's recollection:

> Although I was not a Social Democrat I had friends who belonged to the party. Through them I got the precious work. I read it nights through. It was my own fate and that of thousands of my sisters. Neither in the family nor in public life had I ever heard of all the pain the woman must endure . . . Bebel's book courageously broke with the old secretiveness . . . I read the book not once but ten times. (quoted in Quataert, 1978: 120)

She said the book brought 'hope and joy to live and fight'. When an individual book is so widely influential and directly inspirational, particularly to women, it is important to understand the effect of its argument on the conceptualization of the Woman Question.

Essentially, Bebel confirmed that women's freedom had to wait until after the revolution, that their interests were therefore secondary to the class struggle and their duty was to support that struggle. The duty of socialist women was not to divert energy from the class struggle by autonomous action as women did in what was termed the 'bourgeois' feminist movement. It could be argued that in order to distinguish socialism from its potential rival, feminism, it was important to socialists to challenge the view that sex and class oppression were distinct, or even unrelated, oppressions which demanded separate solutions. It would be too crude to see the socialist construction of the Woman Question as only the pragmatic response of one movement concerned to recruit at the expense of a competing ideology. But part of the complexity of the evolving relationship between socialism and feminism is the nature of the original socialist construction of the Woman Question.

The relationship between sex and class oppression is crucial to socialism's understanding of the Woman Question. The key to this relationship for both Engels and Bebel was the analogy they drew between sex and class. Engel's view was that:

> The first class opposition that appears in history coincides with the development of the antagonism between man and woman in monogamous marriage, and the first class oppression coincides with that of the female sex by the male. (Engels, 1976: 129)

This view was based on this sex/class analogy. It is of primary importance for Engels as it was for Bebel, yet the nature of the original sex antagonism is not made clear; it merely slides into one of class antagonism. For so central a concept, it remains remarkably muddy. It finds its expression in Engels's statements about capitalist society where he says that, 'within the family he is the bourgeois, and the wife represents the proletariat' (Engels, 1976: 137). Thus the economic definitions of class in the wider society are also used to describe relations within the family which are seen as a microcosm of class society. Essentially class and sex oppression are being equated although the nature of this comparison is never examined or made explicit, except that it is assumed that both forms of oppression are at base economic and will together cease only with the end of class society.

Yet class position is defined by relationship to the means of production not to that of reproduction. By using the term 'class' to describe the sexes, the relations of reproduction have become part of the relations of production. As Zillah Eisenstein points out, Engels is assuming that exploitation and oppression are equivalent concepts, yet:

> Exploitation speaks to the economic reality of capitalist class relations for men and women, whereas oppression refers to women and minorities defined within patriarchal, racist, and capitalist relations. Exploitation is what happens to men and women workers in the labour force; woman's oppression occurs from her exploitation as a wage-labourer but also occurs from the relations that define her existence in the patriarchal hierarchy – as mother, domestic labourer, and consumer . . . Oppression is inclusive of exploitation but reflects a more complex reality. (Eisenstein, ed. 1979: 22–3)

Bebel also uses the same approach without further clarifying the nature of the sex/class analogy and its ramifications for socialist theory. He writes:

> Woman was the first human being to come into bondage: she was a slave before the male slave existed. All social dependence and oppression has its roots in the *economic dependence* of the oppressed upon the oppressor. In this condition woman finds herself, from an early day to our own. (Bebel, 1971: 9)

Unelaborated, such statements suggest that there is, at least, a similarity between sex and class oppression and, at most, that one oppression, that of sex, can be subsumed within the wider economic oppression.

Neither Engels nor Bebel fully explores the sex/class analogy which is the linchpin of the argument and it is on these shaky foundations that the edifice is built of socialism's understanding of the Woman Question. It is through the sex/class analogy that women can be integrated into the heart of socialism, its class analysis. Yet it is the use of that analogy which itself precludes the emergence of any developed understanding of women's oppression within socialist thinking. The Woman Question has found a socialist answer by disappearing into the class or Social Question, as it was termed. There is therefore no theoretical space to develop any understanding of patriarchy, as either a separate or a related system, for sex oppression has in effect been rendered invisible.

In order for that sleight of hand to occur, the concept of sex oppression itself had first to be recognized. Ironically, the fact that Bebel accepted the existence of sex oppression (and sought then to compare it with, and then dissolve it into, class oppression) gave a status and recognition to the experiences of women and ensured the acceptance of the Woman Question as a genuine question in its own right. Despite his contention that the Woman Question is part of the wider Social Question, he nevertheless stressed that, 'it is necessary to treat the so-called Woman Question separately' (Bebel, 1971: 1). This then was the ambivalence at the heart of the socialist construction of the Woman Question. Socialist theory both recognized and then effectively shelved the Question. Thus in seeking to identify women's particular oppression, Engels and Bebel had arrived at a point where, undeveloped, their arguments could be used to legitimize very different interpretations of the Woman Question.

By providing a theory in which it was possible to conceptualize the Woman Question, Engels and Bebel set the framework for socialist organizations of the Second International and beyond to develop a relationship with women as potential and actual socialists. No Second International party challenged this orthodoxy on the Woman Question (see Boxer and Quataert, eds., 1978; Evans, 1977) although they differed as to the detail of their practical efforts to recruit women. The extent of the political energy that any one national party was willing to expend on the Woman Question also varied.

From this point onwards, I will look at a particular example, that of the SDF, to extend the discussion into a consideration of the ramifications of Engels's and Bebel's construction of the theory of the Woman Question for that organization's understanding of the question and its consequent approach to women as potential members. With the broader points concerning the theoretical base having been made, it should then be clear that any particular example has resonances for socialism as a whole.

For the SDF, the socialist understanding of the Woman Question in tandem with their narrow economic definition of socialism provided a theoretical basis, and hence endorsement, for an open policy on women's issues and the Woman Question. The SDF as an organization, therefore, contained individuals with a wide range of views in this area who could, at least in terms of socialist theory, be allowed to develop and expound their ideas with impunity. But no particular viewpoint could officially become party policy. The resulting ambivalence had consequences for women's perception of socialism and their participation in the party itself.

An official policy of 'no policy' did not, of course, mean that the Woman Question disappeared from political discussions or the columns of *Justice* and *Social Democrat*, the monthly journal. It did mean that other factors came into play in determining the overall impression of an SDF viewpoint. These necessarily favoured the views of those who already had power and who had access to the media. In particular it explains, if it does not excuse, the amount of space given to Belfort Bax and his supporters, who argued forcibly against any sex/class analogy, proposing not only that women were not oppressed but that they were, in fact, the privileged sex, practically and legally. This it seems could then explain, and even justify, for example, wife-beating as the revenge of the oppressed man:

> If one looks at the matter fairly, one surely cannot be surprised at occasional violence committed on women – wife assaults, wife murders, etc. Legalized tyranny and inequality has always throughout history led to sporadic outbursts of brutality on the side of the victims. It is always so and always will be so. (*Justice*, 27 July 1895)

This was clearly *not* socialist policy but the ambivalence of socialism's relation to the Woman Question meant that such opinions could be viewed as merely idiosyncratic rather than reprehensible.

The status quo policy on the Woman Question was not neutral in effect. The vociferousness and the status of Bax meant that feminists and their supporters within the SDF were quickly forced into a reactive position, which in turn proved very frustrating. As Herbert Burrows explained, when he was accused of failing to rise to Bax's bait once again: 'There are certain things a man does not do, and one of these is to argue with a madman . . .' (*Justice*, 2 November 1895).

Structurally, the lack of access of rank and file women to the socialist press and their negligible representation in the leadership minimized any initial response to Bax and company's ability to determine the parameters of the argument. Over time the lack of an apparently vigorous counter-argument to variations on a theme of misogynism reinforced this position and distanced women, and indeed sympathetic men, from the party. Clearly both women and men were incensed by Bax's arguments which appeared throughout the period. For example Catherine Davidson wrote in 1910:

> If this view be upheld by the SDP[3] then women's place is outside; let our members take their courage in both hands if they believe it and say so. Self respecting women members will then resign. If this view be not upheld, then the columns of *Justice* ought to be closed to anyone who wishes to insult *either* sex. (*Justice*, 9 April 1910)

Similarly men argued against the effect of Bax's continued influence:

> What we do complain of is that he and others should be allowed, month after month and year after year, to insult women generally and his fellow socialist women, in particular in the columns of a socialist press . . . The solution of this matter lies in the hands of the women of the SDP. If any of them were allowed, without let or hinderance, to insult men continually in our press as women are insulted, I, as a man should leave the SDP. (*Justice*, 26 March 1910)

But without a re-evaluation of the socialist perspective on the Woman Question, and the admission of women's emancipation into the heart of socialist doctrine, there could be no advance on *Justice*'s apparently liberal editorial position:

> I do not intend . . . to be a party to creating any division whatever in our ranks about a matter which does not affect the material basis of socialism, and over which, it seems to me, socialists might agree to differ, or at least, discuss calmly and without malice. (*Justice*, 20 February 1897)

This was a position which was built on the ambiguities inherent in the original formulation of socialism's understanding of the Woman Question, which in practice allowed opponents of the Woman Question to determine much of the debate.

In summary, there was a particular combination of theoretical positions which ensured that the Woman Question was not integrated into socialism itself. This combination was the limited economic definition of socialism, which marginalized women, and the theoretical construction of the Woman Question itself which, while paradoxically endorsing the existence of the question as such, sought to bury it within the larger class question. Together they enforced the status quo by providing a theoretical justification for the absence of a party line on the Woman Question for SDF members. This had specific ramifications for their practice and for their perception of women as potential political agents and thus for the process of politicization.

Practice

The most important implication of the socialist construction of the Woman Question, coupled with the SDF's understanding of socialism itself, was that it made a virtue out of the political vacuum it created around women. The Woman Question as a conscience issue provided no measure for socialist practice in relation to women and, as a consequence, allowed all sorts of assumptions about women and political activity not only to surface but actually to gain credibility. It is important for the implications for socialist theory and practice to recognize that this was not purely the result of individual prejudice and misogyny but was rooted in the ambiguities of the theory itself.

Women were seen as a reactionary force in society. There was disagreement as to whether they were naturally or socially conditioned to be conservative, but there was a general fear that women constituted a threat to socialism. This was based more on their 'undue' influence over their husbands or over their children than on their own negative influence on socialist politics. The latter was less of an issue because of women's lack of direct political power, particularly the vote, and hence the emphasis was on their indirect but insidious political influence. This view was not untypical:

In very many instances they hinder men from joining the movement, and keep many, even those who have joined, from taking the active part they otherwise would. (*Justice*, 9 September 1893)

A generalized stereotype emerged which also included the point that:

The vast mass of women would consider a man a terrible bore who spoke to them on politics. The delight of women is to gossip about other people, and a thousand other frivolous things. (*Justice*, 7 October 1893)

But it is not just a picture of indifference or foolish apathy. There is more venom in the stereotype:

For one woman who would strengthen a man's hands in a struggle against injustice, there are twenty who would strike them down. If the women are the greatest sufferers by the present system – which I do not deny – it is but just for they are the greatest sinners. 'Submit, submit', is always their cry to the men. 'What do you think you can do to alter it?', they ask, with a sneer, of any man who tries to rouse his fellows to revolt . . . They dominate the men, and make blacklegs and cowards of them. (*Justice*, 12 May 1894)

In practice, therefore, the conception of woman, either as a socialist's wife (socialists always seem to be men) or as the mother of a potential socialist generation, was a problem for socialism. Far more rarely were women defined primarily as workers; for then, in many socialists' eyes, they become invisible in a proletariat undifferentiated by gender. The problematizing of woman therefore focused on her ability to constitute a brake on male socialist activism. The aim of socialists was to neutralize the brake. It was this perception of women which framed the SDF's attitudes to women's potential politicization.

Despite the problem that women seemed to pose, there was never any question that the SDF, as a socialist party, would have to confront the task of women's politicization. From its inception the SDF took it for granted that a future society would be characterized by sexual equality:

At the very first meeting of the SDF, the first point of our political programme, adult suffrage, was adopted and ever since then that demand has been most earnestly interpreted by all our speakers as meaning the complete freedom, political, social and economical, of women equally with men. (*Justice*, 9 August 1910)

Ritual genuflection towards this idea was commonplace and lip-service, at least, was paid to sexual equality as a basic tenet of socialism. It sometimes produced some rather tortuous arguments. For example, H.M. Hyndman wrote:

> I am quite in favour of an equality of rights between women and men
> though I cannot imagine anytime coming when women will have the same
> rights as men; any more than I can figure to myself men bearing children.
> (*Justice*, 5 April 1884)

Such ambivalence did not enhance the SDF's credibility in this area,
yet pragmatically they recognized that they needed women if
socialism were ever to be achieved. It was admitted in general that,
'without women a movement lacks half its vitality' (*Justice*, 4 July
1891), but more crucially:

> We shall be a long way towards having the next generation chiefly socialist
> if we first make sure of our women. (*Justice*, 27 February 1892)

Thus, although women's support in general was needed, the focus
was in fact much more domestic. SDF men's greatest concern was
with their own womenfolk – mostly wives but also sisters and
daughters – whose tacit if not active support had to be won for the
cause. Although there was no question for the SDF that they wanted
women to become socialists, their conceptualization of women as a
problem gave their approach to women's politicization a particular
emphasis.

The SDF's construction of the Woman Question framed their
approach to making women socialists, for it provided the theoretical
justification for involving women as a group in the project of making
socialism. But as it also provided the space for a stereotyped and
limited view of women, and their potential, to predominate in their
press, the perceived distance between theory and practice on the
Woman Question became a key issue for women and their politicization. The gap between socialist men's theory and practice was
commented upon, and felt profoundly, by socialist women in the
SDF. The same point was made by women in the German and
American socialist movements (see, for example, Quataert, 1978;
Buhle, 1981). For the SDF, Ellen Batten asked what the point was of
socialists saying that they wanted women members:

> when those women who do break the bondage of custom and join the
> Socialists are thought and spoken of contemptuously; as was too often the
> case . . . not only will they not join, but the few who have done so, if it
> were not for their strong belief in the righteousness of the cause and the
> educative influence of time, would be inclined to abandon socialism in
> disgust at the inconsistencies between its preaching and its practice.
> (*Justice*, 30 September 1893)

The language in which women were described, and the frequency
with which the stereotype of woman was lingered over in *Justice* was
resented by women SDF members and potential members. As Mary
E. Boyd said:

No woman objects to just and kindly criticism; but all with a sense of self respect and true love for the noble cause of Socialism must regret the vulgar abuse or still worse insidious innuendoes against her sex which so frequently appear in *Justice*. It is not calculated to induce women to join the organisation, and may alienate some who belong to it already. (*Justice*, 18 April 1896)

This obviously had a profound influence on women's conscious choice on whether to engage in political activity at all. Specifically it affected women's evaluation of the relevance of socialist politics to their own experience and needs. And always these decisions had to be placed within the context of the parameters set by the sexual division of labour, women's responsibilities and expectations.

To summarize, the ambiguities of their theorization of the Woman Question enabled the SDF to stereotype and problematize women with impunity, at least in terms of socialist theory. This in turn affected women's perception of the party and of socialism. It also framed the SDF's approach to women's politicization.

Politicization
How were socialists to be made? The SDF's understanding of the process of politicization was more often implied than stated. Little attention, then as now, was given to the process itself. Nevertheless there does appear to be a model, even if it is not set out as deliberately as the term implies. The model was heavily dependent on the effect of political propaganda on an individual who was already discontented. This would then be combined, to a greater or lesser extent, with the practical impact of, for example, industrial action. Here the key element was the collective experience, so often lacking for many women. Thus the crucial elements were ones of access, hence the SDF's stress on free speech campaigns; campaigns for free secular education and state maintenance for children; the need for a socialist press; socialist candidatures for local government and Parliament as a form of propaganda. This was directed at those who were already 'open-minded'. It was no coincidence that many of the SDF men were self-educated. An individual's participation in a single-issue campaign, such as that for the right to work, could begin the continuum of politicization along which there were stages of recruitment to the party, of education within the party through propaganda work, stretching onto class-consciousness itself.

From this rather crude reconstruction it can be seen that the process of politicization assumed by the SDF understood a very public definition of politics and used methods which depended upon access to public meetings, to demonstrations, and to campaigns. Although this strategy could, and did, reach some women, it was not designed to meet their special needs or to overcome the practical barriers that prevented many women's participation in the public forum. The mechanisms adopted by the party might reach some women who could stop and listen, join campaigns, become propagandists or organizers, yet this seems to have been an incidental benefit in a process principally conceived of as reaching potential male socialists. Despite the SDF's stated view that they needed women if socialism were to ever succeed, the party's conception of the Woman Question led them to see general politicization only in terms of the class rather than as a problem permeated by class and gender difference.

How, then, were women socialists to be made? By conceptualizing women principally as a problem and then failing to recruit them to any significant degree through the traditional model, the SDF was left in a state of bewilderment. In the midst of a long correspondence in *Justice* on 'Women and Socialism', the Tattler wrote in exasperation, 'I love and admire the women – but I can't understand them' (*Justice*, 9 September 1893). This prompted a heartfelt response:

> But the astonishing part of it is, they have so much to say about people of whom they know nothing. Perhaps it pays them best not to understand women. (*Justice*, 5 May 1894)

That, of course, did not stop the use of stereotypes of women, which were premised on the assumption that women as a sex could be generalized about in a way which would never be done for men. The male sex was not dealt with as an undifferentiated mass but would be distinguished through class, trade, political conviction and other assorted adjectives.

Women's politicization was dealt with in a number of ways by the SDF. One of the headings used in *Justice* over another discussion on the problem of socialists' wives indicates one approach, for the title was, 'How to Induce Women to become Socialists'. Men were not to be 'induced' but to be persuaded rationally, yet in the case of women, stereotyped as they were, it was discussed in all seriousness how socialism could be 'sweetened' for their consumption. By playing up to women's supposed trivial, parochial, individualistic natures it was suggested that women's support could be won. The Sage of the Northern Heights, knowing women so well, thought that: 'we ought to dazzle them with the wondrous transformations which will happen around us' (*Justice*, 16 June 1894). He believed that women would find the most appealing aspect of a socialist society to be:

> that in all probability their chief duties would consist of 'shopping' and selecting articles which would beautify themselves and their homes, and

add to the comfort and surroundings of their families . . . shopping, you see, would then be an ecstatic pleasure. (*Justice*, 16 June 1894)

The point was to 'captivate and charm the women with the beauties and possibilities of socialism' (*Justice*, 16 June 1894).

Another approach was, in a sense, to deceive women as to the nature of socialism by attracting them to its social side with the boring politics removed. This position was at times extraordinarily patronizing:

> The only opportunity that a Socialist has of getting women to attend a Socialist gathering is to paint a glowing picture of a tea fight, of a concert where certain celebrity artists will appear, of a soirée and dance where there will be a possibility of witnessing new fashions. (*Justice*, 18 August 1894)

At times a slightly more self-critical view of the meetings themselves was offered:

> It may be that our proceedings at branch meetings are too dull and uninteresting for them; but when Social Democrats see the advisability of brightening their branch meetings and lectures (both indoor and open-air) with Socialist and labour songs and music, we may bid a heartier welcome to our womankind to join us, and to many others besides. (*Justice* 27 February 1892)

But this did not mark a reappraisal of branch practice, guided by the genuine criticisms of women. Even if women found many meetings inaccessible and unwelcoming, so might people too! Rather, the myopic focus continued to be on finding something, other than socialist argument, to win women to the cause.

Any approach to women's politicization was dependent on whether the nature or nurture explanation was sought for the assumed conservatism of women. For those who accepted inherent and immutable differences between the sexes, the stress was on minimizing what was most antipathetic to socialism. Bax, and the others who propounded this view, looked to economic change as a means to influence only woman's surface behaviour; her essential feminine characteristics were beyond influence. Their socialism therefore involved the maintenance of a firm sexual division of labour. Their fear was that if feminism were to be accepted women could accrue direct political power in addition to all the advantages which they believed chivalrous and benevolent men had given women. Bax argued that it was men, not women, who were oppressed (Bax, 1913). Clearly any particular energy directed towards women's politicization was unlikely to come from these quarters.

On the other hand, women explained their sex's 'conservatism' by stressing social conditioning in their description of women's subjection and their confinement to the domestic sphere. They accepted that this had had the effect of limiting women's horizons and practically restricting the possibility of their political participation (see Hunt, 1980, for a development of these points). A wide range of practical suggestions was made by women themselves for alleviating their position in the present, and hence encouraging their politicization, rather than just waiting for after the revolution. Socialist men, it was argued, should 'begin in their own homes' (*Justice*, 23 September 1893). It was suggested that husbands should mind the children so that women could attend meetings and that they could read socialist literature to their wives. Socialist propaganda should be geared to women's interests and needs, through a woman's page and specific leaflets. But most of all they argued that a change of attitude towards women was needed. Yet the parent party's attitudes were not, in the end, the focus for change. How could the party have a change of attitude and practice over this 'conscience' issue when they could not, by definition, have a party position on it? Therefore the SDF's view was that it was women's attitudes which had to be influenced and changed to bring them into the party and socialism.

Education was central to the process of politicization and here it was generally recognized that women were disadvantaged both in a general sense and in terms of any openness to socialist ideas. In effect they were seen as starting back beyond the baseline where men entered this process. Therefore in order to defuse the problem that women posed to the party, as socialists' wives for example, they needed their own education. The Women's Circles, set up in 1904, were to serve this purpose. In the eyes of the parent party their role was clear:

> we are only desirous of interesting and educating women and are endeavouring to lead them into the organisation. (*Justice*, 25 June 1904)

Women, therefore, needed education before they reached the stage at which men automatically entered, that is party membership. In essence the Women's Circles were seen as a 'preparatory school where women can be trained to take their place in the fight' (*Justice*, 28 October 1907). Thus it was thought that remedial education was needed to transform the problem wife into the SDF supporter and socialist. This solution reinforced the idea that it was women who were the problem, rather than socialism and its model of politicization.

Conclusions
Is this just the sorry tale of one socialist party with a blind spot? Julia

Dawson, the women's columnist for *The Clarion*, the popular socialist newspaper, did not believe so:

> The fault lies somewhat, I fear, with the way in which the ILP and SDF meetings are conducted. Sufficient prominence is not given to the fact that women are not only welcome but WANTED. When the women do venture to these, they often meet with such a cold reception that they are not by any means encouraged to come again. (*The Clarion*, 25 January 1896)

The feminist Elizabeth Wolstenholme Elmy agreed:

> It is unquestionably the fact that a very large number of the most earnest and thoughtful women workers of the day, whilst sympathising deeply with every effort towards a just and true socialism, are driven back from cooperation and union with any existing English Socialistic group, by the all but universal failure of male Socialists to recognize *practically* in woman the other half of humanity, with rights absolutely equal to those of the male half.
>
> Theoretically, the several Socialistic groups admit this equality, practically they ignore and deny it. (*Justice*, 25 October 1902)

Similarly, any study of women in other socialist parties in the Second International (e.g. Boxer and Quataert, eds., 1978), including the much more successful SPD women's movement in Germany, does not produce such a very different picture. Nor do we need to limit ourselves to this historical period to recognize the ways in which assumptions about women's potential for politicization still hold (see, for example, Siltanen and Stanworth, eds., 1984).

Indeed, many socialist assumptions about women are still tied to the original formulation of the Woman Question, with all its ambiguities. By asking, 'How are women socialists made?', the dearth of attention to the whole process of politicization is highlighted. Socialists need to consider this aspect of their practice in a more realistic manner, for however detailed the discussion of socialist theory is, it all remains academic without a mass crossing of that 'river of fire'. Women, more than ever, need persuading that that journey is worthwhile. As earlier generations of socialist women found with Hannah Mitchell:[4]

> a lot of the Socialist talk about freedom was only talk and these Socialist young men expected Sunday dinners and huge teas with home-made cakes, potted meats and pies, exactly like their reactionary fellows. (Mitchell, 1977: 96)

As she commented, and as this analysis of socialist attitudes to women's politicization confirms:

> I soon realised that Socialists were not necessarily feminists in spite of the

item in their programme affirming their belief in 'the complete social and economic equality of women with men. (Mitchell, 1977: 99)

Notes

1. Ernest Belfort Bax (1854–1926) was a leading member of the SDF, whose misogynist views were published in the socialist press and in volumes such as *The Fraud of Feminism* (1913). As an avowed anti-feminist and anti-suffragist, his personal views gained a wide audience amongst socialists and beyond. Yet his libertarianism, on which he built his opposition to feminism, paradoxically allowed him to support other women's issues such as free love and the critique of marriage, as can be seen in his arguments around the Edith Lanchester case in 1895.

2. Harry McShane (McShane and Smith, 1978: 35) remembers some socialists reading *Origins of the Family, Private Property and the State* but, interestingly, he argues that they were more interested in tracing the origins of society than they were in the Woman Question. Indeed, 'the other argument passed them by'.

3. The SDF changed its name to the Social Democratic Party (SDP) in 1908. This did not signal any dramatic change in policy, either generally or specifically in relation to the Woman Question.

4. Hannah Mitchell (1871–1946) was an active socialist and feminist in Lancashire. Amongst the organizations she was a member of were the Women's Social and Political Union, Women's Freedom League and the Independent Labour Party (including being a Labour City Councillor in Manchester).

References

Barrett, Michele (1980) *Women's Oppression Today: Problems in Marxist Feminist Analysis*. London: Verso.

Bax, Ernest Belfort (1913) *The Fraud of Feminism*. London: Grant Richards.

Bebel, August (1971) *Woman under Socialism*. New York: Schocken Books (first published in 1879; reprint of translation by Daniel De Leon, 1904).

Boxer, Marilyn and Jean Quataert (eds) (1978) *Socialist Women: European Socialist Feminism in the Nineteenth and Early Twentieth Centuries*. New York: Elsevier.

Buhle, Mari Jo (1981) *Women and American Socialism 1870–1920*. Illinois: University of Illinois Press.

The Clarion.

Collins, Henry (1971) 'The Marxism of the Social Democratic Federation', pp. 47–69 in Asa Briggs and John Saville (eds), *Essays in Labour History 1886–1923*. London: Macmillan.

Coward, Rosalind (1983) *Patriarchal Precedents: Sexuality and Social Relations*. London: Routledge.

Eisenstein, Zillah R. (ed.) (1979) *Capitalist Patriarchy and the Case for Socialist Feminism*. New York: Monthly Review Press.

Engels, Friedrich (1976) *The Origins of the Family, Private Property and the State*. London: Lawrence & Wishart (first published 1884).

Evans, Richard (1977) *The Feminists: Women's Emancipation Movements in Europe, America and Australasia 1840–1920*. London: Croom Helm.

Hunt, Karen (1980) 'Women and the Social Democratic Federation: Some Notes on Lancashire', *North West Labour History Society Bulletin*, 7: 49–64.

Jaggar, Alison M. (1983) *Feminist Politics and Human Nature*. Brighton: Harvester.

Justice.

McShane, Harry and Joan Smith (1978) *Harry McShane: No Mean Fighter*. London: Pluto.

Meyer, Alfred G. (1977) 'Marxism and the Women's Movement', pp. 85–112 in Dorothy Atkinson, Alexander Dallin and Gail Warshofsky Lapidus (eds), *Women in Russia*. Stanford, CA: Stanford University Press.

Mitchell, Hannah (1977) *The Hard Way Up*. London: Virago.

Quataert, Jean (1978) 'Unequal Partners in an Uneasy Alliance: Women and the Working Class in Imperial Germany', pp. 112–45 in Marilyn Boxer and Jean Quataert (eds), *Socialist Women: European Socialist Feminism in the Nineteenth and Early Twentieth Centuries*. New York: Elsevier.

Sargent, Lydia (ed.) (1981) *Women and Revolution: A Discussion of the Unhappy Marriage of Marxism and Feminism*. London: Pluto.

Siltanen, Janet and Michelle Stanworth (eds) (1984) *Women and the Public Sphere*. London: Hutchinson.

Social Democrat.

Spender, Dale (ed.) (1983) *Feminist Theorists*. London: The Women's Press.

Stacey, Margaret and Marion Price (1981) *Women, Power and Politics*. London: Tavistock.

Stanley, Liz and Sue Wise (1983) *Breaking Out: Feminist Consciousness and Feminist Research*. London: Routledge.

Steinberg, Hans-Josef (1976) '"Workers" Libraries in Germany before 1914', *History Workshop*, 1: 166–80.

Thompson, E.P. (1977) *William Morris: Romantic to Revolutionary*. London: Merlin.

Tsuzuki, Chushichi (1961) *H.M. Hyndman and British Socialism*. London: Oxford University Press.

Vogel, Lise (1983) *Marxism and the Oppression of Women*. London: Pluto.

III
FEMINIST PERSPECTIVES ON THE NEW RIGHT

4
Patriarchy, capitalism and the New Right

Tessa ten Tusscher

Preface

Since the 1960s British and American feminists working within socialist political groups have provided a sustained and poignant critique of the Marxist consideration of the 'Woman Question'. Women have systematically argued that gender relations cannot be subsumed under the categories of class and the economy and that an autonomous or semi-autonomous body of theory needs to be developed to explain the domination of women by men. There is now an excellent and substantial amount of feminist political theory both addressing the inadequacies of Marxism when dealing with gender, and offering various attempts at a synthesis between Marxism and feminism.

However, with a few exceptions, most western socialist feminist theory has been confined to specific questions about women's lived experience under capitalism and to the significance of women's subordination for the maintenance of capitalist social relations. This chapter results from a fear that feminist political theory risks becoming ghettoized since it does not frequently address questions on the level of macro-politics. This means that nearly all the material available on contemporary mainstream politics is written by men from an unreconstructed male perspective.

I believe that feminists need to capture the political arena both theoretically and politically. Feminist political theory is only of value if it is of use to the political project of ending women's subordination. The object of this chapter is to convert the political theory of the dual-systems explanation of capitalist patriarchy into a methodology for explaining the New Right, and thereby to highlight the nature of the contemporary right which I take to be a serious threat to any socialist and/or feminist.

The aims of the chapter are three-fold. The first is to highlight the failure of the British left to understand the nature of the New Right through their gender-blind analyses. The second is to offer an account of the New Right which puts women, rather than men, at the centre of the stage. This acts not only to counterweight the bulk of male-stream analyses which the left has offered, but also to provide a radically different conceptualization of contemporary politics. Thirdly, this chapter is an attempt to test the viability of the dual-systems theory by using it as a methodology to explain a phenomenon central to mainstream politics.

These aims are ambitious and are offered within the spirit of sisterhood which is the energy which fuels women's political theory and political practice.

Over the last few years, political scientists of all persuasions have turned their attention to what has variously been called the New Right, Thatcherism, radical conservatism or neo-liberalism. There is now an abundance of literature on the subject and anybody attempting to offer an account which they feel to be new or to be an insight not already explored in depth must proceed with caution. On first sight it appears that the New Right has been dissected from every possible perspective and that every component of its ideology and policy has come under scrutiny.

In this chapter I argue that this is not the case and that an essential element of the package which constitutes the New Right or Thatcherism[1] has been systematically either ignored or marginalized. I make what might appear to be an arrogant criticism of the literature. I propose to demonstrate that it all suffers from the flaw (so prevalent within political science) of not making gender relations central to the analysis. As a result the debate around the New Right has become moribund – stuck in a treadmill of male-defined analyses offering male answers to male questions on what has become the dominant force in contemporary western politics. This gender bias has led to a partial explanation of the New Right – on the left, one couched in economic and class terms – which fails to explain (and indeed lacks the analytical tools to be able to explain) the moral/traditional/familial aspects of the present administration's ideology and policies.

Within British political science, there is a lively debate on the left which centres around the characterization of Thatcherism and around explanations for its emergence. This chapter is offered as a contribution to the debate, although it is hoped that it will also be of interest both to those who occupy another part of the political spectrum, and to those whose interests do not lie solely within the realm of British politics.

Before going on to offer a feminist analysis of Thatcherism, I will give a brief survey of the competing orthodoxies within Marxism. The intention is to highlight how these theorists have either ignored gender relations or else have fudged the issue of patriarchy within their analyses.

The left's view of the New Right

Among the 'hard-left' the view prevails that Thatcherism is merely an expression of capitalism in crisis. According to this view there is nothing new or distinct about the New Right; it is merely the current example of the chain of reaction which directly serves the interests of the ruling class. In this vein David Beecham, of the Socialist Workers Party, sees the Conservative Party as the direct agent of the capitalist class. It articulates its interests, is personed by its members and operates solely for the interests of employers. The New Right is analysed solely in terms of its offensive against labour in its attempt to raise the level of exploitation. In short, it is a 'perfectly understandable strategy for British capitalism' (Beecham, 1983: 4). This strand of Marxism is impatient with ideas around ideology and would regard the content of this chapter as part of 'bourgeois feminist deviationism'. It insists on analysing politics purely in terms of the economy and exclusively by reference to actual policies pursued against working class organizations. Ironically, this is reminiscent of the American positivist tradition which only analyses conflict when it is actually being articulated, and thereby ignores the more subtle political practices which set the terrain of acceptable policies and which determine the range of conflicts to reach the political agenda (Lukes, 1974).

Stuart Hall pinpoints the major problem with developing a form of analysis which operates solely at the level of the economic base when he says 'It is predicated on the view that a social formation is a simple structure in which economic contradictions will be immediately, transparently and indifferently translated onto the political and ideological stage' (Hall, 1983: 21). Hence any discussion of the specific nature of the British crisis in the 1980s is ignored and therefore any discussion of the specific political experience of different classes, races and genders is silenced.

Standing at the opposite end of the Marxist continuum is the view that Thatcherism must be seen as a political strategy; as 'a response by the right to a *political* stalemate which is seen as standing at the heart of the British crisis' (Glynn and Harrison, 1980: 135–47). Arguing in a similar vein, Geoff Hodgson characterizes Thatcherism as a set of 'value judgements' rather than as a coherent economic strategy. Central to these political judgements is the conception of freedom based on the right of individual contract and on private property. As the free market is viewed by the right to be the epitome of freedom, state intervention is rejected. Equally, taxation is curbed because it is understood to be a denial of voluntary contract. Government spending creates distortions in the free market and is consequently viewed as a limitation on freedom. Trade unions are seen to deny the freedom of the worker to negotiate individual contracts, and inflation, acting as a debaser of currency, is defined as a form of involuntary taxation. As Hodgson says:

> Here described in ideological terms, is the obsession with the control of inflation; it is to preserve, as much as possible, an idealized market economy, where money is a reliable store of value, and to minimise government intervention in that hallowed realm of freedom. Here explained is the passion for tax cuts, unfounded as it is on any positivist theory of evidence and the crusade to reduce government intervention in the economy. Here explained are the attempts to limit the powers of trade unions and to make trade union action less effective. (1981: 182)

Thus, for Hodgson, the economic base pales into insignificance in the face of an autonomous ideology of the ruling class. At one stage of his argument he characterizes the New Right as nineteenth-century liberalism and suggests that its adoption by the capitalist class represents some kind of false consciousness within the bourgeoisie as it does not represent the ideology most suited to its long-term interests. As Michael Bleaney says, he views Thatcherism as 'ideology run riot so that it no longer responds to reality but pursues its blinkered course regardless of where it culminates' (1983: 132).

For the purposes of this discussion, the most interesting facet of this type of analysis is its gender-blindness. Thatcherism may view individual contract as an essential element within its economic perspective; however, the concept of freedom from constraint is a freedom to be restored for *men*. For women, the ideology of the New Right is based on a denial of our newly found economic and political freedoms. (This point will be taken up in more detail later in this chapter.)

A third way of characterizing the New Right is to view it as a form of 'creeping fascism'. This is, perhaps, the least theorized approach but it is one (particularly since the coercive apparatus of the state became so apparent during the recent British miners' strike) which is gaining increasing support from many left activists. This characterization highlights the tendency towards authoritarianism of the British state demonstrated by the extensions of police powers; the increased reverence for militarism; the erosion of civil liberties through telephone tapping, the Police Act, harassment of young blacks; the strong leadership which Thatcher exerts over the Conservative Party and; the assaults on trade unions, most notably GCHQ[2] and the National Union of Mineworkers. However, as both Hall (1983) and Jessop et al. (1984) point out, it is a mistake to equate the New Right with fascism because it can only be understood as a form of passive transition rather than as a mass mobilization. There are no economic or political organizations which actively support the project. As Jessop et al. ask:

> Where are the Thatcherite 'new model' unions, the Tebbit Labour Front, the Thatcherite Youth, the women's movement, Thatcherite sports leagues, rambling clubs etc, which might consolidate and fix a mobilised working class? (1984: 43)

This sort of analysis tends to be simplistic and invokes the socialist to stop theorizing and to 'see the writing on the wall'. The left is urged either to take to the streets and confront the state or to form political alliances with any anti-Thatcher movements in a bid to defeat the present administration and restore the conditions for social democracy.

There have been two interesting spin-offs from the 'creeping fascist' debate. Firstly, there has been an attempt to offer a psychoanalytic perspective on the appeal of the New Right which is reminiscent of Reich's study of Hitler (Reich, 1970). This psychological explanation sees the support for Thatcher as emanating from the repressed sexuality of the British male (West London Socialist Society, 1983). Secondly, there has also been the emergence of a feminist analysis of the New Right which equates this creeping fascism with patriarchy. Sheila Ruth suggests the possibility of such a perspective when she says:

> Fascism, fully revealed, is the extreme, exquisite, expression of masculism, of patriarchy, and thus the natural enemy of feminism, its quintessential opposite . . . Fascism, authoritarianism, the New Right are three facets of the same reality – unchecked Patriarchy. (1983: 350)

Not surprisingly, Ruth's argument has not been taken up by the left. I would suggest that it is refutable on the same grounds as those made previously. The assertion that the New Right can be equated with fascism is simplistic and fails to deal with the complexity of the social formation of contemporary western societies. However, it is interesting that this approach, which is the least orientated towards a narrow understanding of the economy, should be the one which gives some space for a feminist perspective.

Finally, there is the form of analysis prevalent in *Marxism Today*. Stemming from Stuart Hall's (1983) notion of authoritarian populism (which in turn is strongly influenced by Gramsci's (1971) notion of hegemony), this view insists that the crisis facing British capitalism is organic. In order to understand the crisis, all the conjunctural aspects need to be situated in their proper relationship. For Hall, the immediate terrain of struggle is not merely the given economic conditions but 'the incessant and persistent efforts which are being made to preserve the status quo' (1983: 23). These efforts are formative, aiming at a new balance of forces – a new historic bloc 'with new political configurations and philosophies, a profound restructuring of the state and the ideological discourses which construct the crisis and represent it as it is "lived" as practical reality – a new sort of settlement' (1983: 23).

While not denying the relevance of the economic crisis (or more specifically the decay of the post-war consensus under conservative hegemony in the 1950s and the subsequent failure of a labourist, corporatist alternative), Hall argues that many of the key themes of the radical right pre-date the economic crisis. They emerged as a response to the radicalism of the 1960s and must be understood as part of the struggle for consensus within the dominant bloc. The electoral success of Thatcherism is explained within the contradictions of social democracy, which in times of economic crisis forces social democratic parties to play conflicting roles of managing the crisis within the logic of capitalism while defending working class interests. According to Hall, the failure of the Labour Party to perform this task between 1974 and 1979 in Britain left the space for Thatcherism, or for authoritarian populism.

Authoritarian populism is a complicated and, some would say, an ambiguous term, implying a convergence between the demands of those in authority with the pleas by the populace for a solution to the present crisis. As Jessop et al. (1984: 34–6) point out, Hall's interpretation varies between a view of authoritarian populism as an exceptional form of the capitalist state, as the routinization of coercion to secure consent or, more simply, as the articulation of a new type of political project with popular support.

The populist elements are easy to identify. Firstly, there is the identification of the essential British character as 'strong', 'free-thinking' and 'individualistic'; not in need of a 'soft' 'coddling' state. (It is here that the 'scrounger' is installed as the antithesis of the true Brit.) Secondly, there are the resonant themes of organic Toryism which Andrew Gamble highlights (1983): themes of nation, the family, duty and order. These are combined with aggressive neo-liberal sentiments of self-interest, competition, and anti-statism; in short, the free economy and the strong state (Gamble 1979: 132–64). Thirdly, there is the language of the new cold war, with virulent anti-

Sovietism combined with the perils of 'Red Ken' and the Greater London Council, 'Commissar' Scargill and the pro-Soviet Greenham women[3] jointly threatening the very fabric of British society.

Despite the variations in these approaches, they share certain common assumptions. They all agree that the New Right has become a dominant political force as a result of some sort of crisis in capitalism. While Stuart Hall and Andrew Gamble both condemn the 'hard left' for its simplistic view that the ideological and political realms operate as mirror images of the economic base, both share its view that the underlying problem is one of capital.

For Beecham, the so-called shift to the right is mere ideology destined to be blown away when economic forces exert their absolute determinancy. Capitalism is in crisis – it is a crisis of production and is one which is reaching a crescendo. The class struggle is becoming harder because 'there are two sides of the class struggle and the other is beginning to realise it is fighting to survive' (Beecham 1980: 1). Hence we are faced with a 'last ditch attempt to reconstruct the economy and to switch class forces back in favour of capital'. In contrast, Glynn and Harrison (1980) (of the autonomous ideology school) see the New Right as a package of conditions aimed at increasing surplus value. While Bill Jordan (1982) analyses it in the context of the inability of national governments to restore productivity in the face of the demands of international capital, Stuart Hall and the writers of *Marxism Today* talk about Thatcherism as a product of a particular historic conjuncture where three trends converged. First is the long-term structural decline of the British economy along with the deepening world recession. Second is the collapse of the social democratic consensus. Third is the resumption of the new cold war. The debate within the British left centres on defining the nature of the crisis, analyzing the relative autonomy of ideology, and determining the relationship between class, ideology, the state and the economy.

Feminist critique of left analyses of the New Right
In the United States there is a growing body of literature which analyses the American New Right from a radically different perspective. Feminists have taken seriously the assertions of the Moral Majority that the success of Reagan depends on its moralism and its hostility to feminism. As one of the leaders of the Moral Majority proclaimed:

> It was the social issues which got us this far, and that is what will take us into the future. We never really won until we began stressing issues like bussing, abortion, school prayer and gun control. We talked about the sanctity of free enterprise, about the Communist onslaught until we were

blue in the face. But we didn't start winning in elections until we got down to gut level issues. (cited in Davis, 1981)

Feminist theorists have placed the moral/familial components of the New Right at the heart of their analysis of Reaganism and (to a more limited extent, of Thatcherism). As Zillah Eisenstein (1981) says of the US experience and as Miriam David (1983) reiterates for Britain, it is these moral issues which distinguish the political parties of the New Right from the old right. Marxist writings on the subject have either totally ignored these moral/familial issues or have analysed them as part of an ill-defined concept of populism. Stuart Hall appears to view family ideology as part of the populism of Thatcherism. However, he fails to explain why ideology hostile to women's freedom should be popular or whether there is a differential gender base for this element of populism. The approach of the hard left, which sees family policy as part of the ideology of the New Right aimed at obscuring its true project of dismantling the welfare state and increasing the reserve army of labour, fails to explain why it should be women who bear the brunt of the Thatcher onslaught. Gamble's analysis, which sees Thatcherism as a combination of the social market economic strategy and 'the more congenial Conservative emphasis on a stronger state in the fields of defence, law and order and a strengthened family' (1983: 119), while attractive on its own terms, fails to examine why a patriarchal family is congenial to conservatism or why the right-wing of the Tory Party should take to it with such enthusiasm.

Traditionally Marxism has not been happy with a view of politics which focuses on gender relations and on reproduction. It tends either to consign them to part of the ideological superstructure or to analyse them as an effect rather than a cause. In the rest of this chapter I will offer a view of Thatcherism which escapes the class reductionism of orthodox Marxism and which accounts for the New Right's attitude towards women and for the centrality of its sexism to its politics.

The socialist feminism of Heidi Hartman (1981) and the dual-systems school offers the most illuminating approach to the study of capitalist patriarchy. Here patriarchy is defined as:

> a set of social relations between men, which have a material base, and which, although hierarchical, establish and create interdependence and solidarity among men which enable them to dominate women. Though patriarchy is hierarchical and men of different classes, races, or ethnic groups have different places in the patriarchy, they also are united in their shared relationship of dominance of their women; they are dependent on each other to maintain that dominance. (Hartman, 1981: 14–15)

The material base lies in men's control of women's labour power. This is maintained by the two-fold restrictions of women's access to the labour market and on women's sexuality. While the institutions of control vary over different historical eras and through divergent cultures, in western capitalist societies the family and the institution of monogamous marriage stand out as a particularly efficient control mechanism. For many socialist feminists (e.g. Barrett, 1980) the monogamous family occupies the site of male domination over women because it acts to control access to resources and to determine women's sexuality as reproducers and pleasers of men, thereby restricting women's access to paid labour. Patriarchal relations are also enforced outside the family. Women are excluded and marginalized from the labour force through a host of practices which include sexual harassment at the workplace, rape, lack of provision of child care and trade union exclusionary practices. These are reinforced through images of women as 'sexy', the 'whore' or the 'housewife', perpetrated by the media and pornography industries. Child rearing is essential for the maintenance of patriarchy in precisely the same way that reproduction of labour power is necessary for capitalism. Patriarchal social relations are reproduced through children being reared by the unpaid labour of women who are defined as socially inferior; they are maintained and reinforced through the churches, the education system, the health service, the institutions of recreational sport and the state. Thus the material base of patriarchy lies both in heterosexual monogamous marriage and in all the institutions which control womens' access to paid labour.

Hartman (1981) argues that there is both a gender and a class dynamic to history. There are times when patriarchy is functional to capitalism (as, for example, by providing a reserve army of labour or through the provision by women of the reproduction of labour power), and there are times when they stand in contradiction. They certainly cannot be collapsed into each other. The tendency of Marxism to conflate gender relations into the categories of economic classes indicates the source of its weakness. This flaw has hampered Marxist analyses of the New Right, for by refusing to see gender as a force in history which operates at a level of autonomy from class dynamics, Marxism has been forced to relegate the moral/familial component of the New Right to the margins.

Stuart Hall (1983) points out that many of the elements of the ideology of the New Right developed before the crisis of social democracy became apparent. Andrew Gamble (1979) informs us that Thatcherism has a long intellectual history. However, neither analyst offers reasons to explain why the non-economic aspects of the ideology should come to the fore when they did. Hall equates Thatcherism with a backlash against the challenge to the established order by the ferment of 1968, by the student riots, the alliances between student and worker, and the hippie movement. I would suggest that his refusal to acknowledge the significance of the changing position of women since the 1950s highlights the weakness of a methodology which does not embrace patriarchy.

The crisis of patriarchy
The changing position of women is of major significance in the establishment of a sufficient characterization of the New Right. During the 1960s women were gaining control over their reproduction, the capitalist boom was drawing more and more women into the paid workforce, women were entering trade unions at a faster rate than men were, the growth of higher education institutions was promising women access to the professions and, after a forty-year lull, the women's liberation movement was mushrooming. Women were demanding the right to have abortions, within the political realm they were insisting on the right to organize autonomously, the women's movement was highlighting the depths of sexism which permeated both the public and the private sphere, and many women were rejecting the institution of monogamous heterosexual marriage. In short, patriarchy was perceived to be in crisis and the material base of men's control of women's labour power was under threat.

It was this crisis of patriarchy which promoted the birth of the moral right. Both inside and outside the Conservative Party, lobbies, organizations and groups of 'concerned adults' were reacting against the tide of feminism. Mary Whitehouse and her National Viewers and Listeners Association (see Tracey and Morrison, 1979), the Festival of Light, elements within the National Association of Freedom and other middle class associations, and the organized church were recoiling with horror against the growth of the so-called permissive society and the sexual revolution. Working women were blamed for juvenile delinquency and the rising crime rate. The media capitalized on the theme of 'latch-key' children, social scientists bemoaned the breakdown of the family and predicted the concomitant breakdown of order and morality. The anti-abortion lobby started its campaign against 'a woman's right to choose' and launched a virulent defence of the 'Right to Life'.

However, during the 1960s the climate was not ripe for the revival of patriarchal forces. The demands of patriarchy were conflicting with those of capitalism. Women's sexual liberation was being commodified, there were vast profits to be made from the wage packets of the newly socially productive woman. During this period capitalism was contending with the problem of stimulating consumption and wage-earning women were able to perform the economically desirable function of consuming the commodities produced during the boom. This relative economic freedom conflicted with the needs of patriarchy and was perceived as a threat to patriarchal structures. If men could no longer fully control women's access to paid labour and if women were gaining control of their own fertility through contraception or abortion, then the material base of patriarchy was under threat.

By the early 1970s (and increasingly through this decade) the economic crisis facing capitalism became ever more deep. This crisis gave the space for the moral right to link back into class politics and to reassert the reunited interests of capital and patriarchy.

Thus, Thatcherism and the New Right managed to occupy the vacuum created by the breakdown of social democracy combined with the opening stemming from the perceived threat to patriarchy. This determined the nature of the New Right. It embraced the twin goals of restoring class forces in favour of capital and of restoring gender relations in favour of men. While the parallels between the United States and Britain can easily be overstated, George McGovern's comment on the election of Reagan is pertinent to Thatcher's victory.

> The family issues raised by the right wing was a code word for putting women back into the kitchen, stripping them of any decision on the question of abortion, and forcing them back into the old orthodox ways. (quoted by Eisenstein, 1981: 191)

It has been argued that to draw parallels between the Moral Majority in the United States and the moral right in Britain is to misunderstand the nature of the British right. These arguments tend to take two forms. Firstly, there is the simplistic assertion that, as Britain has a female Prime Minister, and as Thatcherism has a very strong personal stamp emanating from Margaret Thatcher, then the Conservative Party success at the polls indicates a victory for British feminism. This position has been argued by some sections within the 300 Group who see *any* woman in a position of power as a victory for feminism, but it represents a misunderstanding of the issue.[4] As I shall show later, Thatcher has done nothing to advance the position of women. On the contrary, since the election of 1979 women have suffered sustained and repeated attacks on their economic and reproductive freedoms. Thatcher's image and the rhetoric of Thatcherism are fully consonant with the restoration and maintenance of patriarchal gender relations. As she says, feminists

> have become far too strident and have done damage to the cause of

women by making us out to be something we're not. You get on because you have the right talents. (Thatcher, 1978)

and:

I am absolutely satisfied that there is nothing more you can do by changing the law to do away with discrimination. After all, I don't think there's been a great deal of discrimination against women for years. (Thatcher, 1981a)

Gender relations, or patriarchy, are not dependent on the gender of the head of government. They are structural issues, not solely matters of individuals or interpersonal relations.

A more sustainable critique of the perspective which sees the New Right as anti-feminist has been made by Lynne Segal writing in *Marxism Today* (1983). She argues that, while it may have produced certain policies which indirectly disadvantage women, overall Thatcherism has been ambivalent in its attitude towards women's rights. In an article arguing that Thatcherism is not the Moral Majority and is not a general offensive against women, she equates the relative lack of success of the anti-feminist right with the strength of the British women's movement. While I agree with the heart of Segal's argument that the New Right has been forced to contend with the opposition of the British women's movement, there is little within her analysis to demonstrate that its intentions are not anti-feminist. Clearly, their relative lack of success is related to the strength of opposition which can be generated by the women's movement. It is also true that the US women's movement has been far more successful than its British counterpart in affecting legislative changes in favour of women's rights, due to the method of operating of the National Organization of Women which has organized within the mainstream of American political life. This is a totally different strategy from the one adopted by British feminists, who have largely steered clear of parliamentary politics and have shunned attempts to voice a women's caucus within party politics.

The centrality of the National Organization of Women within the American system has left open a space for the anti-feminist right to attack American feminism in an overtly political manner. The Moral Majority and the various pro-family groupings successfully campaigned against the Equal Rights Amendment and actively debated the Family Protection Act in Congress. On the surface this would seem to distinguish the (explicitly anti-feminist) American right from its British counterpart which has not launched similar anti-feminist statutes. But, as Miriam David (1983) points out, British legislation relating to women's rights is much weaker than its American counterpart. There is no legal commitment to positive discrimination, the Equal Opportunities Commission is an institution which uses persuasion rather than litigation, and feminism in Britain has not entered the mainstream political agenda. Instead, British feminism has exerted pressure in a more vicarious manner, forcing the moral right to adopt more subtle and complex strategies to exert patriarchal relations.

Thatcherism does not need to revoke the Sex Discrimination Act or the Equal Pay Act as neither of these pieces of legislation offers a serious challenge to sexual inequalities in the labour market. However, the Conservatives have launched a general offensive against women's rights. This has consisted of a twin-pronged attack on women's sexuality and on their access to scarce resources.

The government has made plain its intentions to uphold 'traditional family values'. Its Family Policy Group's prescriptions, leaked in 1982, were designed to 'seek ways of counteracting those factors which tend to undermine, or even prohibit, the exercise of personal responsibility and a sense of individual self-respect'.[5] These included policies aimed at shifting responsibility for social and public services away from the government towards the family, thereby following the ideology of the moral right that 'God designed the family to take care of people from the cradle to the grave. The state is no substitute' (quoted in Marshall, 1985: 36). The Family Policy Group's suggestions included: the encouragement of mothers to stay at home, the promotion of schools with a clear moral base, the privatization of aspects of the personal social services and the encouragement of private provision for social needs, the shifting of responsibility for anti-social behaviour of children onto parents and the encouragement of self-help among the unemployed.

Implicit in the prescriptions is an understanding of the 'family' which both maintains the sexual division of labour and prescribes that the caring and servicing roles should fall upon the woman. The family is construed as the bastion of decency and morality. As Thatcher said in Parliament:

> Most people want to reassert the true values of the family and society. They recognize the role of the family and the school in bringing up a new generation which responds to law and accepts the need for order. (Thatcher, 1981b)

Concurring with the ideas of the Family Policy Group, Rhodes Boyson, Minister for Social Security, in a speech outlining the government's intention to pay greater attention to moral issues, blamed parents for the present social crisis. As Miriam David points out, he laid

> the responsibility for rioting youths, football hooligans and murderous

muggings on the sins committed by the parents of today's disillusioned youth. (1983: 40)

More specifically, it is mothers who are blamed for rises in the levels of promiscuity, drug abuse and juvenile crime. Women combining motherhood with paid employment are given responsibility for social disorder. As Thatcher put it:

> It is possible, in my view, for a woman to run a home and continue with her career provided two conditions are fulfilled. First, her husband must be in sympathy with her wish to do another job. Secondly, where there is a young family, the joint incomes of husband and wife must be sufficient to employ a first class nanny-housekeeper to look after things in the wife's absence. The second is the key to the whole plan. (Thatcher, 1960)

The New Right's reaction against women's freedoms does not exist solely at the level of ideology. Since 1979, there has been a steady flow of legislation which endorses these views and a host of policies which attack women's sexual and economic liberty.

The success of the economic offensive is demonstrated by current patterns of women's employment which, as Sylvia Walby (1983) points out, mirror the conflicts between patriarchy and capital. Since the mid-1970s women's official rate of unemployment has increased by a factor of five while men's has increased by a factor of two. In fact, the disparity is even greater since many married women do not register, particularly since 1982 when claimants have had to pass an 'availability test' for unemployment benefit which includes a form asking for proof that adequate arrangements have been made for the care of children and dependants. For women, unemployment represents not only poverty, but also the intensification of patriarchal relations and a reduction in the ability to shift some of the burden of housework either onto her partner or onto socialized methods.

The Thatcher government has been instrumental in increasing women's unemployment through the reduction of personal social services, thereby forcing women to stay at home and look after dependants. As Geoffrey Finsberg said when justifying cuts in nursery provision:

> I do not see it as the state's job to say that the parents of young children should or should not work. This is the parents' decision. But they should recognize their responsibility for their children's welfare when making that decision. (quoted in David, 1983: 41)[6]

In addition to increasing levels of unemployment, there has been another important element in the restructuring of the labour market which has ramifications for the relationship between patriarchy and capital. The massive increase in levels of part-time work (usually undertaken by women) has been of benefit both to capital and to patriarchy. Capital benefits because part-timers, since the 1982 Employment Protection Act, lack protection against dismissal. Part-timers are usually the first to lose their jobs and constitute the reserve army of labour as they are more flexible than full-timers. Part-time work also offers little threat to patriarchal relations because, firstly, the wages are sufficiently low to maintain the woman's dependence on the man's income and, secondly, because the woman is still capable of offering the full servicing duties required within patriarchal relationships.

Thus, as Walby points out, the restructuring of the labour market endorsed and furthered by the New Right has produced a situation beneficial to both patriarchy and capital. As she says, 'Maybe the fit between patriarchy and capitalism is neater and tighter than ever before' (1983: 111).

In addition to the economic offensive, there have also been attacks on women's sexuality. The recent victory by Victoria Gillick banning contraception for the under 16s without parental consent has given confidence to the moral right,[7] and was rapidly followed by intense lobbying of MPs by the anti-Warnock lobby on the issues of surrogacy and reproductive technology.[8] Since the Gillick verdict, teachers, doctors, social workers and health workers have been besieged with letters and admonitions to restore 'traditional family values'. A member of one of the moral right groups was recently reported as saying:

> I am very optimistic about the way things are going. Some education authorities are stopping their sex-education classes to under 16's. Many of those lessons, teaching contraception are in fact advocating child sex. The Family Planning Association has had to withdraw its leaflets to the young. (Riches, 1985)

The right has a history of campaigning against sex education in schools and has made demands for parental censorship of classes as well as for the promotion of the Whitehouse notion that 'the only good sex is marital sex'.[9] Following the prescriptions of the moral right, the Health Education Council in 1982 launched a campaign to stop unwanted pregnancies, not with advice about contraception, but through stressing young women's responsibility for morality with the slogan 'girls should say no, boys should think first' (see David, 1983: 39).

There has also been a long and concerted campaign by SPUC and LIFE to criminalize abortion.[10] Although these issues are always given a free vote when debated in the Commons, the moral right always has turned out in force to show their support. In a recent article, it has been suggested that there is a moral whip developing within the Conservative Party, consisting of forty Catholic MPs and a number of fundamentalist Protestants, which promotes the moral lobby (Toynbee, 1985).

The moral right's adherents consist not only of extra-parliamentary groupings, but also of leading philosophers within the Conservative Party. Roger Scruton argues that contraception 'has effectively severed the sexual act from the generative tendency' (1985). He opposes reproductive technology because it threatens the sanctity of motherhood.

> In surrogate motherhood the relation between the mother and child ceases to issue from the very body of the mother and is severed from the experience of incarnation. The bond between the mother and child is demystified, made clear, intelligible, scientific – and also provisional. (1985)

Rhodes Boyson and Sir Keith Joseph, Minister of Education, concur on the need for 'moral education' and 'preparation for parenthood and adult role in the community' through courses which would:

> help pupils to recognise the importance of those human relationships which sustain, and are sustained by family life and the demands and duties that fall on parents. (David, 1983: 40)

John Gummer, the former Chairman of the Conservative Party, has implied that these sorts of courses should replace education promoting anti-sexism and anti-racism (1985). This emphasis on 'moralism' is part of a broader trend, aiming to restore patriarchal relations. It is a more subtle offensive against feminism than the explicit anti-feminism of the American right – but it is an equally potent one.

Thatcherism and the New Right can only be understood if this gender dimension is taken into account. The failure of Marxist theorists to take on board feminist analytical tools has rendered their conceptualization of the New Right partial and incomplete. Marxists frequently respond to feminist critiques defensively, characterizing gender politics as standing in opposition to class. This does not necessarily have to be the case. Socialist feminism, which gives weight to both gender and class, offers Marxism a richness which it ignores to its own detriment.

Conclusions

The emergence of the New Right can only be explained within the context of crises of both social democracy and the economy, combined with a crisis in patriarchy. This sort of analysis does not involve the rejection of a Marxist framework. It merely demands that another dynamic be taken on board. I agree wholeheartedly with

Hall's proposition that Thatcherism is an attempt to redraw the political map (1982) – an attempt to reconstitute class forces in favour of the oppressors. Further, the analysis which argues that it is on the terrain of the conjuncture that the forces of opposition must organize, appears as an obvious truth. If the conjuncture is understood as 'the coming together of often distinct though related contradictions, moving according to different tempos, but condensed in the same historical moment' (Hall, 1983: 21), then there is no apparent reason why the related contradictions cannot be those between capital and labour and between men and women. This would offer an explanation of why the New Right emerged, of its form and its appeal. It would also provide some guidance on how to organize against the right, which must remain the purpose underpinning any radical analysis.

Notes

1. While being fully aware of the nature and significance of the debate around the naming of the phenomenon variously termed Thatcherism, the New Right, neo-liberalism, radical conservatism, in this chapter I will use the terms loosely. This choice has been made in order to highlight the varying terminology of the different analysts considered. It is not a statement about my own position within the debate. Personally, I prefer not to use the term Thatcherism because I feel that it personifies a set of policies and ideologies and thereby tends to oversimplify the problematic. However, I find the concept of radical conservatism to be unsuitable since I can find no elements of radicalism within the ideology of the present government. Neo-liberalism is equally problematic since, particularly in their attitudes to women there is little which can be characterized as liberal or new. This leaves me with the term New Right, which, as Zillah Eisenstein and Miriam David point out, can imply that it is the moral issues which distinguish the New Right from the old right and therefore seems most useful within the context of this discussion.

2. In 1984 the Thatcher government banned trade unions at the government's General Communications Head Quarters at Cheltenham.

3. In 1985 the Thatcher government abolished the Greater London Council, the elected body for the whole of London, of which 'Red Ken' (Ken Livingstone) was leader of the Labour majority. Arthur Scargill is President of the National Union of Mineworkers, whom he led in the miners' strike of 1984–5. The 'Greenham' women are peace protesters who since 1981 have camped in an all-women's protest outside the Greenham Common airbase, where Cruise missiles are sited.

4. The '300 Group' is a voluntary association of women whose aim is primarily to attain the election of 300 women Members of Parliament (half the total number of MPs, to represent half the total population).

5. The Family Policy Group, set up by the Thatcher government, comprised a number of cabinet ministers, civil servants and Conservative Party advisers. Although it operated in secret, reports were leaked to the press (see *The Guardian*, 17.2.83).

6. Geoffrey Finsberg was Under Secretary of State for Health and Social Security, 1981–3.

7. Victoria Gillick won an Appeal Court decision to prohibit the prescribing of

contraception to women under 16 years old without parental consent. The decision was subsequently overthrown in 1985 by the Law Lords.

8. Dame Mary Warnock chaired a committee set up by the Thatcher government to consider and make recommendations on in vitro fertilization and surrogate motherhood. (Cmnd. 9314, *Report of the Committee of Inquiry into Human Fertilisation and Embryology*, July 1984)

9. Mary Whitehouse set up the National Viewers and Listeners Association to campaign against sexual explicitness on television and in favour of censorship of pornography in print, film or video form.

10. SPUC – the Society for the Protection of the Unborn Child – is a predominantly Roman Catholic backed association which, together with the organization LIFE, campaigns against abortion.

References

Barrett, Michele (1980) *Women's Oppression Today: Problems in Marxist Feminist Analysis*. London: Verso.

Beecham, David (1980) 'The Ruling Class Offensive', *International Socialism*, 6(4): 1–18.

Beecham, David (1983) 'Get the Tories Out', *Socialist Review*, 54(2): 3–6.

Bleaney, Michael (1983) 'Conservative Economic Strategy', pp. 132–47 in Stuart Hall and Martin Jacques (eds), *The Politics of Thatcherism*. London: Lawrence & Wishart.

David, Miriam (1983) 'The New Right in the USA and Britain: A New Anti-Feminist Moral Economy', *Critical Social Policy*, 2(3): 21–45.

Davis, Michael (1981) 'The New Right's Road to Power', *New Left Review*, 128: 28–49.

Eisenstein, Zillah (1981) 'Antifeminism in the Politics and Election of 1980', *Feminist Studies*, 7(2): 187–205.

Gamble, Andrew (1979) 'The Free Economy and the Strong State: The Rise of the Social Market Economy', *Socialist Register*, 1–25.

Gamble, Andrew (1983) 'Thatcherism and Conservative Politics', pp. 109–31 in Stuart Hall and Martin Jacques (eds), *The Politics of Thatcherism*. London: Lawrence & Wishart.

Glynn, Andrew and John Harrison (1980) *The British Economic Disaster*. London: Pluto.

Gramsci, A. (1971) *Selections from the Prison Notebook of Antonio Gramsci*, Q. Hoare and J. Nowell Smith (eds and trans). London: Lawrence & Wishart.

Gummer, John (1985) personal correspondence with the author.

Hall, Stuart (1982) 'Redrawing the Political Map', *Marxism Today*, December: 14–20.

Hall, Stuart (1983) 'The Great Moving Right Show' pp. 19–39 in Stuart Hall and Martin Jacques (eds), *The Politics of Thatcherism*. London: Lawrence & Wishart.

Hartmann, Heidi (1981) 'The Unhappy Marriage of Marxism and Feminism', pp. 1–41 in Lydia Sargent (ed.), *Women and Revolution: A Discussion of the Unhappy Marriage of Marxism and Feminism*. London: Pluto.

Hodgson, Geoff (1981) *Labour at the Crossroads*. Oxford: Martin Robertson.

Jessop, Bob, Kevin Bonnett, Simon Bromley and Tom Ling (1984) 'Authoritarian Populism, Two Nations, and Thatcherism', *New Left Review*, 147: 32–61.

Jordan, Bill (1982) *Mass Unemployment and the Future of Britain*. Oxford: Blackwell.

Lukes, Steven (1974) *Power: A Radical View*. London: Macmillan.

Marshall, Kate (1985) *Moral Panics and Victorian Values*, London: Junius.

Reich, Wilhelm (1970) *The Mass Psychology of Fascism*, London: Souvenir Press (first published 1946).

Riches, Valerie (1985) reported in *The Guardian*, 17.6.85.

Ruth, Sheila (1983) 'A Feminist Analysis of the New Right', *Womens Studies International Forum*, 6 (4): 345–51.

Scruton, Roger (1985) *The Times*, 5.2.85.

Segal, Lynne (1983) 'The Heat in the Kitchen', pp. 207–15 in Stuart Hall and Martin Jacques (eds), *The Politics of Thatcherism*. London: Lawrence & Wishart.

Thatcher, Margaret (1960) *London Evening News*, 25.2.60.

Thatcher, Margaret (1978) *The Times*, 10.5.78.

Thatcher, Margaret (1981a) *Thames Television News*, 6.1.81.

Thatcher, Margaret (1981b) *Hansard*, 4.11.81.

Toynbee, Polly (1985) 'The Catholic Whip which Cracks the Rest of us into Line', *The Guardian*, 17.6.85.

Tracey, Michael and David Morrison (1979) *Whitehouse*. London: Macmillan.

Walby, Sylvia (1983) 'Women's Unemployment, Patriarchy and Capitalism', *Socialist Economic Review*, 99–114.

West London Socialist Society (1983) *The Mass Psychology of Thatcherism*. London: Socialist Society.

5
Women and neo-liberalism

Georgina Waylen

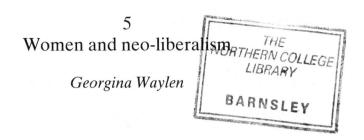

Preface

Within the feminist spectrum there are a wide-ranging variety of views on how a feminist political theory can best be achieved. Firstly, there is the view that existing theories can be read more sensitively. Secondly, another view is that women can be added in to essentially unproblematic theories, as it is the subject matter rather than the methodology or assumptions that is limited. Thirdly, some assert that a simple integration is difficult or impossible to achieve because the methodology and range of assumptions upon which much of political theory is based makes it impossible to include women, as the coherence of the theories cannot be maintained if a serious attempt to integrate women is made.

This chapter fits into the third of these perspectives. It demonstrates that by using a feminist analysis (range of assumptions and so on) to look at neo-liberalism, it can be shown that neo-liberal ideas are based on certain ideas about women, and that the coherence of the model can only be maintained if women are not considered as individuals, but are instead subsumed elsewhere under the family. Not only does neo-liberalism miss women out; because of its underlying assumptions about women, it also becomes impossible to put women back in as individuals, as this would entail a radical restructuring of the theories and destroy the foundations of neo-liberalism. Feminists would therefore reject neo-liberalism because of both its theoretical basis and its practical implications (the intensification of the subordination of women). This makes neo-liberalism the antithesis of the ideas of the women's movement.

These characteristics are not confined to neo-liberalism, but are common to much of political theory as it is at the moment. Thus this chapter has the more general relevance of demonstrating that there is a need to build a feminist political theory. This does not mean that *all* theories, methodologies and concepts should be ignored, but that there should be a radical reassessment of what political theory can tell feminists, and that a feminist political theory should be reconstructed with gender as a key concept. There is, for example, a need to redefine concepts such as justice and equality, combined with a need to challenge and refute theories such as neo-liberalism.

The rise in the popularity of neo-liberalism means that it is necessary to develop some critical analysis of these ideas. Their superficial attractiveness, and the appeal of popularized versions to common-sense notions prevalent within society, conceal a deeply ideological programme which entails maintaining and increasing the subordination of women.[1] A challenge to the underlying philosophical assumptions within the model is necessary. The purpose of this chapter is two-fold: firstly, to attempt to highlight some of the fundamental incoherencies and logical inconsistencies within the model itself; and, secondly, to show that the promise of neo-liberalism can never be delivered. If neo-liberal prescriptions are put into practice, liberty can never be something enjoyed by all the population, and the 'best' ordering of society using existing knowledge giving everyone the best chance of doing well and accruing a higher income could never be achieved.

Flaws within the model can be discerned from a variety of perspectives; this chapter seeks to highlight some of the ways in which a feminist analysis can illuminate an understanding of neo-liberalism. An attempt will be made to show that the neo-liberal vision of the world is misconceived – it does not portray social reality as it is – and that there are contradictions within the model when attempts are made to reconcile what is with what it is felt there should be. These factors make it possible to demonstrate that implementation of the prescriptions of neo-liberalism will not achieve the desired ends.

In its apparently genderless conception of society, neo-liberalism has much in common with a great deal of western political thought. Women are hardly mentioned in the work of the neo-liberals. Indeed this sort of critique of neo-liberalism helps to illuminate much of what is at fault with political theory in general, and is also a good illustration of other criticisms of neo-liberalism. Feminist analyses in general challenge the basis of political philosophy itself and much of social science theorizing. Alison Jaggar (1983: 21) has written that contemporary political philosophers have said very little on women, and suggests that this implies either that standard moral or political theories apply without modification to women or that they do not apply to women at all. Furthermore, from the silence of contemporary philosophers one could infer either that there are no differences between women and men that are relevant to political philosophy, or that women are not part of the subject matter of political philosophy at all. It would be ridiculous to claim that there are no relevant differences when feminists argue that every aspect of social life is governed by gender, so that it becomes impossible within present-day society to claim that women are treated the same as men in any sphere of life, and yet most political philosophers would not want to claim that women were irrelevant to their studies. Further to this it can be argued that in the case of neo-liberalism, while women are not discussed in any detail, neo-liberal ideas are based on certain assumptions about women and the coherence of the model can only be maintained if women are left out as individuals and subsumed elsewhere under the family.

In order to demonstrate this it is necessary to highlight some of the basic ideas of neo-liberalism before demonstrating their inconsistencies and showing what the results of neo-liberal policies for women would be in practice. This outline will obviously be very cursory and will not emphasize some features which are crucially important in a different context.

To look at neo-liberalism it is necessary to go back to first principles and consider how human nature and society are theorized. This is difficult as there is no definitive theorist. I will look at Friedman and Hayek, as the best known.

Both have similar prescriptions but arrive at these from very different conceptual starting points. Hayek has a more rigorous philosophical basis for his theorizing than does Friedman, who appears more concerned with mechanisms than with underlying principles. This is perhaps why Hayek's work appears more coherent than Friedman's. These differences are shown in the methodologies they use, which both stem from and affect their particular conceptions of the problems they address.

Friedman is a positivist, believing that social science should use the same methods as natural science, as it too deals with phenomena which can be objectively known and tested by statistical methods. Friedman (1953) believes that one reason for minimizing interference in the economy is a lack of knowledge about its workings at present, but he believes that it is perfectly possible and likely that knowledge will increase in the future. Hayek has a totally different approach – characterized by Brittan (1980) as a subjectivist and axiomatic philosophy of social science – much influenced by the Austrian school. Hayek (1967a, 1967b) believes that the methods of physical science are inappropriate for social science. He makes a critique of bogus quantification, because the phenomena involved are too complex for simple quantitative regularities between economic variables to be discovered. This is not because of the insufficient development of economic theory, but because of the fundamental difficulty of obtaining any complex explanation of highly complex phenomena. Theories are not therefore to predict specific outcomes (such as the numerical level of prices) but to describe the general character of the order which will form, which can still be empirically tested. Hayek's views on complex phenomena are extended in his beliefs about human knowledge in general, the significance of which will become apparent.

Since they begin from different methodological starting points, Friedman and Hayek are bound to have different reasons for advocating the same outcomes. Despite this I feel it is better to look at them together rather than separately, concentrating on Hayek and contrasting Friedman to him when he is saying something which appears very different.

Obviously both Friedman and Hayek are trying to delineate a system which will guarantee the best ordering of society.[2] Hayek believes that this will be achieved through 'liberty' as 'that condition of men in which coercion of some by others is reduced as much as possible in society' (1960: 11). Liberty is not just an end in itself but the source and condition of most moral values. As an extension of his views on the complexity of phenomena, Hayek believes that 'the case for individual freedom rests chiefly on the recognition of the inevitable ignorance of all of us concerning a great many factors' (1960: 29). Liberty therefore becomes essential to leave room for the unforeseeable and unpredictable, as the scientific methods of the search for knowledge are not capable of satisfying all of society's need for explicit knowledge. This means that no man or group of men possess the capacity to determine the conclusive potentialities of other human beings.

Indeed, an extension of this is Hayek's belief, put forward in his 'Principles of a Liberal Social Order', that liberty derives from:

> the discovery of a self generating or spontaneous order in social affairs
> . . . an order which made it possible to utilize the knowledge and skill of
> all members of society to a much greater extent than is possible in any
> order created by central direction. (1967c: 162)

An order of a much more complex set of facts is achieved than could ever happen by deliberate arrangement. These ordering forces are the regularity of the conduct of the members.

This spontaneous order is desirable because it has no purpose, nor does it need agreement concerning concrete results: it merely allows every individual to use the knowledge he has to his own best advantage. It is based on reciprocity or mutual benefits arising from the free market. Hayek (1967c) believes that it is misleading to call this an economy, as an economy is a deliberate arrangement of a given stock of resources or organization in the service of a unitary order of purpose. Hayek calls the spontaneous order a 'catallaxy', as there is no single hierarchy of ends.

Hayek's conception of liberty therefore necessarily entails economic freedom, but the underlying concept goes back one stage further. Friedman (1976: 13), on the other hand, seems to identify his concept of freedom much more closely with simple economic freedom, and seems to see the market much more in terms of the allocation of resources enabling everyone to get what they want, as in the example of the red and green ties. It is, as he says, a 'dollar for dollar' arrangement comprising the voluntary co-operation of individuals – it is this which constitutes true freedom. Coercion is therefore prevented within the market by individuals acting as consumers, able to buy from more than one seller, and as employees able to sell their labour power to more than one employer and vice versa – hence its voluntary nature. This definition of coercion and liberty is therefore inseparable from the concept of the private domain of the individual and therefore the material side of this private domain – private property.

The implications of Hayek's views are that human society as it is now has not been created by the deliberate actions of human beings. From this it is clear that Hayek (1945: 44) is critical of liberal ideas associated with 'cartesian rationalism'. Freedom (Hayek, 1960: 54) itself is an 'artefact of civilization' but did not arise from design. Once it did result, and people realized this, they perfected it. Hayek believes that people who think they can affect society do so because they view the human mind as being independent of its environment and culture, which is untrue. He believes that there are two factors – innate genetic rules, and cultural rules – which both affect the human mind.

Why then is government necessary in this spontaneous order? Both Friedman and Hayek recognize that some limited form of government is necessary. Friedman (1962) has a simplistic and pragmatic view which is in terms of dealing with exigencies of circumstance. The 'problem' of social organization is as much to prevent bad people from doing harm as it is to enable good people to do good. Thus government does something the market cannot do for itself; that is, determine, arbitrate and enforce the 'rules of the game'. Indeed Friedman claims that

> the organisation of economic activity through voluntary exchange presumes that we have provided through government for the main-tenance of law and order to prevent the coercion of one individual by another, the enforcement of contracts voluntarily entered into, the defin-ition of the meaning of property rights, the interpretation and enforcement of such rights and the provision of a monetary framework. (1962: 27)

Hayek's emphasis (1967c) is different, concentrating on the rule of law as the most important factor, with some form of government as the necessary corollary of this rather than an end in itself. A free society (Hayek, 1967c: 163) has to be nomocratic, that is, law-governed, as this 'extends the possibility of peaceful co-existence of men for mutual benefit beyond a small group whose members have concrete common purposes'. This was only possible:

> by the extension of purpose independent (formal) rules of just conduct . . . rules which did not impose obligations for particular actions . . . they consisted solely in prohibitions from infringing the protected domain of each which these rules enable us to determine. (Hayek, 1967c: 165)

Hayek (1967c) therefore wishes to restrict the coercive powers of government to the enforcement of just rules of conduct. This implies a great distinction between the 'rule of law' required for a spontaneous order (which necessitates the universal applicability of these rules and means that it is impossible to decide the justice of any particular rule except within the framework of the whole system of such rules), and the particular commands issued by an authority for the purpose of organization. This type of coercive act of government, if laid down by general rules, does not have such a deleterious effect on individual freedom as one might expect, since the general rules become data on which the individual can base his own plans.

What then are the implications of these views on liberty which are relevant to this chapter? Because of the emphasis here, crucial implications are ignored which would receive detailed consideration in another context – particularly those which are more obviously concerned with the public sphere, such as the ideal form of government and the role of trade unions.[3]

For the purpose of this discussion there seem to be three significant results. Firstly, one of the aims of liberty is to ensure that the protected domain of law, liberty and property is as large as possible for individuals. One can only infer that the domestic sphere falls somewhere within this protected domain from Hayek's (1979) rather vague description of what it entails (property defined to include not only material things). The implications of this location will become apparent later.

The second important implication of Hayek's view concerns the concept of social justice. According to Hayek this concept is the basis of much of the present 'welfare statism' that threatens to undermine the workings of the spontaneous order, because it brings about a change from a liberal society to a totalitarian one, and the rules of just conduct become obscured and replaced by the rules of organization of government.

This welfare statism arose (Hayek, 1967c) because it was realized that the application of equal uniform rules results in different consequences and differences in material position. The desire to combat this led to a new concept of justice: social or distributive justice, that is, wanting particular results for particular people, which can only be achieved by a purpose-governed organization. Hayek believes that the concept of social justice is fallacious, as justice can only be attributed to human action, and not to outcomes which have not been deliberately brought about by anyone. Since the results of the catallaxy are unpredictable, it is ridiculous to describe its results as unjust or immoral, and thus there can be no test or criteria for social justice. Criteria for social justice are also impossible because they would imply some kind of agreement regarding desired ends, which would not exist in a spontaneous order. The attempt to achieve social justice turns the spontaneous order into an organization, that is, totalitarianism. Not only does it destroy individual freedom, it is also a mirage which could never be achieved as there is no agreement on the relative importance of different ends.

It has to be remembered that Hayek (1960) warns that the market does not bring a close correspondence between subjective merit and individual needs and rewards. It is a combined game of chance and skill. For each individual the results are determined to an extent by circumstances beyond his control. According to Hayek, if people agree to enter into the spontaneous order, they have to agree to abide by its outcome. Hayek argues that one of the main factors which brought 'social justice' to the fore was the demand for protection against an undeserved descent from an already achieved position. However, the position someone had before was no more deserved than the one they have now. It can therefore be seen that while Hayek believes that, on average, people in a catallaxy will be better off, there is no guarantee that this will happen to all; indeed, it seems almost inevitable that some will do badly. This is unavoidable, and cannot even be judged in moral terms as it is an unintended rather than deliberate consequence of human action. Friedman (1963) has a rather simplistic critique of the welfare state, which basically is that it is an attempt to do good at someone else's expense. 'Nobody spends other peoples' money as carefully as they spend their own' (1976: 11). If doing good also requires taking money away from people, this entails coercion and a destruction of freedom.

The policy prescriptions arising from these views are generally well known, and need only be listed briefly here. Obviously there has to be a reduction in the welfare state although both Friedman and Hayek believe that there should be some mechanism to deal with those who 'fall below'.

Friedman (1963) seems to believe that the freer the market the greater the role private charity would play, citing the example of the nineteenth century as the era of the most unrestricted operation of the free market and the greatest burst of charitable activity. In practical terms he realizes that some kind of provision would have to be made. He advocates a form of negative taxation, so as to preserve the incentive for people to better themselves.

Hayek believes that in a society as rich as modern society (he does not specify whether this includes third world countries) there is no reason why some minimum security should not be provided outside the market for those who 'fall below'. Hayek (1960) also believes that it is reasonable that some degree of coercion is needed to ensure that people make provision for bad times. This is compatible with liberty, if this type of insurance is through private contractual arrangement, since if people do not make preparations for hard times their upkeep will impinge on others. The danger of a monopolistic government service is that it can act according to the principle of allocation according to need and therefore becomes a deliberate transfer of income from one group to another. Hayek therefore believes that a state pension system becomes a form of coercion of the young by the old. Hayek (1960) also does not believe in a free health service as this leads to great resources being spent on people who will never contribute to society again. People should therefore insure themselves according to how much treatment they want. In the case of unemployment, there is a need for some basic provision but this should not be above the minimum as the cure for unemployment requires flexibility of wages and mobility of workers, both of which are reduced by high unemployment provision. Overall the market should be able to operate as freely as possible. This also entails removing the monopoly privileges of trade unions and deregulating the labour market.[4] (Business monopolies are not seen as being as detrimental.) All this is enforced by strong but limited government.

The third implication of Hayek's concepts of liberty and general rules applicable to all is that there are few circumstances where there can be special rules which apply to particular classes of people, and then only if they possess properties which others do not. Hayek (1960: 154) refers to these simply in terms of biological characteristics; for women this means that there would be some special rules, such as with regard to rape, and childbirth.

Friedman considers discrimination in terms of race; if necessary these ideas can be extended to women. Friedman can have no explanation for discrimination within his framework and so implies that it is irrational behaviour, as the people who practise it are the losers by denying themselves opportunities, for example through refusing to work with black people. Significantly, discrimination is only consi-

dered in terms of the economic market. Friedman believes that the
solution lies with

> the impersonal market which separates economic activities from political
> views, and protects men from being discriminated against in their
> economic activities for reasons irrelevant to their productivity. (1962: 21)

The example Friedman gives is of wheat growing – nobody knows
who grows the wheat, therefore they do not ever consider
discriminating. Parallels can be drawn here between this economistic
analysis and that of Marx and Engels, who believed that discrimination against women would end as they entered the labour market
as wage labourers. The neo-liberal argument must therefore be that
in a free market there would be no discrimination against women
(whether this would extend to 'natural' differences resulting in
different working conditions can be speculated upon). There would
also be no justification for any positive discrimination in favour of
any groups or individuals, as everyone has to be equal in front of the
law. Specific laws relating to women's biological characteristics are
the only overt consideration that Friedman and Hayek appear to give
to women. It is, however, the fundamental assumptions they make
about women within their framework which are the most significant.
Before discussing this it would be useful to consider briefly the libertarian feminist case as it demonstrates an attempt to combine neo-
liberalism and women's *rights*, based on the view that within the free
market there would be no discrimination against women.

Judy Barnes (n.d.) claims that there is a need for special attention
to women's *rights*, because of three basic groups of problems which
need to be overcome for women to achieve liberty. The first of these
is governmental discrimination – such as protective laws involving
work, which provide an excuse for not hiring women for certain jobs
or not giving them a chance at overtime – and governmental laws
treating women as a class, such as alimony and custody of children
based on a particular idea of a woman's role. The solution to this is to
reduce laws which 'discriminate' against women; that is, all laws
referring to women. The second problem is institutional discrimination: discrimination by employers. This can be removed by greater
competition as only large monopolistic firms can afford not to hire
according to ability – using sex as a criteria, for example.

The third problem is interpersonal discriminatory behaviour. This
is recognized as the most important, and basically consists of the
socialization of women and discrimination in personal interactions.
The answer to this is the implementation of the first two sets of
prescriptions, plus individualistic solutions, for example raising
children as individuals. True to form, women are urged to 'not give

sanction for mistreatment of yourself – or others' (Barnes, n.d.). Learning assertiveness is one answer. Having removed discrimination in terms of laws and in the market it is then up to the woman to 'take the responsibility to be free' (Barnes, n.d.). Therefore what the free market cannot guarantee is up to the individual women themselves to achieve, as it would be unwise to try and force those who discriminate not to do so.

While it would be possible to criticize neo-liberals on the basis of the little they do say about women and discrimination in general, it is necessary to explore what ideas about women are implicit in their work before a full critique can be made. Neo-liberals' overt silence about women does not mean that women do not have a particular role to play within the neo-liberal vision of the world.

Since women are often subsumed under the family in many theoretical models, it is reasonable to infer that when the family is discussed this is generally a euphemism for women's role within the family and beyond that within society, as it is women who perform the roles associated with 'the family'. Neo-liberals use a consideration of the family common to other sorts of analysis. Milton Friedman writes: 'The ultimate operative unit in society is the family. The acceptance of the family as the unit rests in considerable part on expediency rather than principle' (1962: 3). The family, then, is seen by implication as a natural unit, and a residual category. There is no need to explain its nature or existence as these are seen as self-evident, nor is there any need to question its role or ask whether it should carry on in its present form.

The role which the family is supposed to play reveals what sort of family is conceptualized. Milton Friedman believes that government should only supplement private charity and the private family in protecting the irresponsible. When combined with Hayek's view of the family as the place of socialization and instillation of society's values, this would seem to imply that the family unit is conceptualized as consisting of a working husband and a non-working wife, whose attention is devoted to looking after children and other members not capable of looking after themselves – the sick and the old.

The family is, therefore, seen as a basic unit of society (although this is not stressed because of the obvious contradiction with the conception of society as composed of individuals). The sphere of the family is to be left outside government control within the protected domain and private sphere. Hayek writes that:

> The conditions of domestic service like all intimate relations, offer opportunities for coercion of a particularly oppressive kind . . . Society can do little to protect the individual beyond making such associations truly voluntary. Any attempt to regulate these intimate associations would

involve such far-reaching restrictions on choice and conduct as to produce even greater coercion: if people are free to choose their associates and intimates, the coercion that arises from voluntary association cannot be the concern of government. (1960: 138)

The implication of Hayek's view is that once people have married of their own free will, legislation and the state have little role to play in the regulation of domestic life and the private sphere in general.

There has therefore been no coherent statement about women by neo-liberals, although much can be surmised from the implications of their basic schema. However, one disciple has written a history of the family from within this type of framework. While it gives no prescriptions as to policies towards women and families, it gives another example of the type of attitudes which are held about the family and the role of the private domain. Ferdinand Mount (1982) believes that over the last one thousand years the family has proved not to be a carrier of the ideas of the state and church but, on the contrary, to have been one institution which has prevented the tyranny of the church and state in unison, and which has upheld the values of liberty – hence the title of his book, *The Subversive Family*. He also takes great pains to show that, contrary to (his rather ill-informed rendition of) feminist ideas, women are not oppressed within the family.

What then are the implications of this model for women? It is clear that while neo-liberals have very little to say about women (except for stating the need to have laws regarding women's particular 'biological' capacities) it is necessary to look beneath what is said, to what is not said. Like many other variants of political theory and social analysis in general, neo-liberalism depends on a number of assumptions about women which form a fundamental part of the whole model. It is these assumptions which give the model a logical inconsistency, and yet are necessary in practical terms. Like other strands of liberalism, this model is attempting to delineate prescriptions to guarantee the liberty of the individual, and yet the assumptions about the role of women in the family are in no way consistent with a recognition of women as individuals.

Neo-liberals subsume women within the family and the private sphere. There is obviously a contradiction here: on the one hand, individuals are the basic units of society, interacting in the free market, but, on the other hand, it is only the male head of the household who behaves as an individual. Barrett and MacIntosh (1982) claim that the conflation of the individual and the family is absolutely necessary for the model; since it is argued that both the individual *and* the family is the basic unit of society, this contradiction can only be overcome by uniting the two. This has to be done in order to elevate the doctrine of the free market into an entire social ethic.

This means that all members of society who do not enter the market must be ignored, which is done by subsuming them, as members of families, into the individualism of the head of the household, who can then be assumed to be the economic agent. It is then possible to believe that the whole economy is organized on the liberal individualist model of the free market, with everyone working in order to support themselves, and with those who cannot subsumed under those who can.

How therefore are women to be seen? As individuals in their own right, or subsumed under a male head of household? The main implication of this conflation of neo-liberalism is that the doctrine of the individual becomes the doctrine of the male, as the sex which can enjoy the 'rights' and 'privileges' of the free market. Indeed the free market can only function if women are not considered as individuals. This becomes very clear when the implications of neo-liberal policies are considered. Hayek's rejection of concepts of social justice and welfare statism means that the private family should take the burden of caring for the irresponsible and incapable. It is not the individual male head of household but the woman within the family who should care for the children, the aged, and the mentally and physically handicapped, in the absence of state provision. Neo-liberalism is therefore incoherent even within its own parameters: it talks of liberty for all individuals, but in reality only advocates it for men. Indeed, it works on the assumption that women are not individuals.

Moving outside the internal inconsistency of the neo-liberal model, it is possible to demonstrate that its vision of the world is overly simplistic and misconceived. The libertarian feminists demonstrate this when they are forced to recognize that even if the free market were working perfectly and all 'discriminatory' legislation had been removed and rules of just conduct introduced, there would still be interpersonal discriminatory behaviour. They can have no coherent explanation or solutions for this within their framework apart from exhorting women to take their own freedom as individuals. This is an implicit recognition that there are other factors which combine to subordinate women.

A feminist critique is in some senses parallel to a Marxist one. Both recognize that neo-liberalism is not grounded in reality but an idealized and highly ideological view of the world used to justify a certain social order. However, the world is not and can not be full of individuals competing equally within the free market in the way seen by neo-liberals. Andrew Gamble, as a Marxist, argues that the most important defect of this type of liberal political economy is its handling of capital, particularly:

in its failure to perceive how radically the structure of the market economy is transformed by first the emergence and then the development of capital within it. (1979: 17)

The significance of this is that to the importance of individual exchange (which is supposed to be paramount) is added another dimension – that of capital accumulation. Some of these independent producers and merchants become capitalists buying labour power, organizing production and selling commodities. This means that the market economy changes qualitatively. The most significant change for Gamble is the emergence of two different classes which now confront each other in production: one which has only its labour power to sell, and the other capitalist class which owns the means of production. This leads to exploitation of the workers by capitalists and makes a mockery of the argument that through organization of the free market everyone has the chance to do as well as anyone else.

This critique by Gamble highlights other general questions about neo-liberal analysis, particularly its static and universal nature. There is no concept of historical specificity and change. This kind of approach can be paralleled by feminists. Not only are individuals not competing in the free market on equal terms because they are divided into workers and capitalists with different resources. In the same way, men and women are not equal individuals: there are unequal relations of power and oppression between men and women. The structural and institutional inequalities rooted in society could not be removed by instituting equal legal status for women.

Feminists (e.g. Beechey, 1979) see women's subordination as something more fundamental and profound than mere discrimination, hence the use of the concept of patriarchy. Political theory is therefore both a reflection of and justification for this. A feminist analysis of society and women's oppression (e.g. Barrett, 1981; Hartmann, 1981; Kuhn and Wolpe, 1978; Edholm et al., 1977) is obviously a task too large to be undertaken in a chapter of this nature. It is possible only to point to a few salient factors which are important in this context. Much of women's oppression is predicated on what is conceived of as women's 'natural' role in reproduction; that is, the extension of biological reproduction to social reproduction – a feature common to neo-liberal analysis with its assumptions about women within the family. These ideas play a large part in the ideological construction of gender, of what is considered to be the female nature and role. This conceptualization of women's role within the private sphere also affects women's role in the public sphere. Contrary to the underlying assumption of neo-liberals that women are in the private domain and therefore do not enter the labour market, women do, but not on the same terms as men. Historically there has been a tendency for women to perform jobs which are seen as an extension of their domestic role both within the professions and in 'unskilled' work in caring, nursing and servicing roles.

The dominant conceptualization of women's role within the private sphere has therefore played a large part in the subordination of women in both the public and private sphere. This is illustrated in the neo-liberal idea of the protected domain. Hayek and Friedman consider it to be very separate from the public sphere where the outside world has no right to interfere. However, in this idealized vision of the protected domain, neo-liberalism misrepresents the position of women in numerous ways, both conceptually and empirically, which leads to some ambivalence in terms of practical policies. Conceptually the neo-liberal concentration (common to other basically economistic forms of analysis such as the Marxist concentration on production) on exchange and the market, as being the only type of 'economic' activity, is another example of a simplistic analysis drawing a veil over the way the economy and society work. The links between women's role in the home and production in the classic sense are ignored, and the false separation between the private and public spheres is reinforced. Within neo-liberalism the conceptual separation between production and reproduction obscures the role women play in subsidizing costs for capital: if reproduction occurs within the family and is undertaken by women outside the wage labour market then the value of labour power is reduced and surplus value increased.

Centrally for feminists the neo-liberal conceptualization of the nature of the private sphere is the antithesis of their analyses. If men and women are not equal individuals, the idea of the undesirability of intervention in the domestic sphere means that unequal relations of power between men and women can continue without any hindrance. The idea of the inviolable private life just obscures the nature of relations within this sphere. There can be no sphere where social relations and power structures are absent or irrelevant. The neo-liberal separation between the public and private means that issues such as rape in marriage, domestic violence and pornography become non-issues. These are all issues which feminists believe it is necessary to campaign against; indeed feminists would argue that the private sphere cannot be depoliticized and removed from the arena of debate, which is what neo-liberals are advocating.[5] An understanding of the neo-liberal conceptualization of the nature of the public/private dimension and women's position within it is vital in any attempt to comprehend the fundamental assumptions on which these models are based and the ways in which they ideologically bolster women's oppression.

The contradictions and oversimplifications inherent within the neo-liberal model (women are not treated as individuals but are subsumed within 'the family', along with the idealized view of the economy) mean that the practical implications of the policy prescriptions of neo-liberalism are not those intended in the model. One obvious implication of the vision of women within the domestic sphere is that it is desirable for women to leave the labour market and return to the home because of the reduced levels of social provision. However, the example of Chile tells a different story. In post-1973 Chile the implementation of Chicago School policies, particularly the reduction in social services, and increased levels of poverty caused by unemployment, has put greater burdens on women, particularly working class women. This has been coupled with effects of the restructuring of the economy, which has led to a relative increase in women's employment in the service and informal sector. Women have therefore been pushed back into the labour market through dire necessity and have congregated in those sectors which have historically absorbed the greatest number of women. Despite the lack of empirical evidence, it can therefore be surmised that women's oppression has qualitatively increased under this Chicago School model, within the spheres of both production and reproduction. Further investigation needs to be carried out as to the precise effects upon women's lives, especially within the sphere of reproduction, looking at the rigidity of the sexual division of labour in the context of high male unemployment, and the concrete ways in which the reduction of social provision has affected women's tasks in the home.[6]

It can therefore be argued that neo-liberalism does not just leave women out of its analysis; the whole model is based on assumptions of a certain role for women. Women are not considered as individuals but are subsumed within the family and therefore could not enjoy the neo-liberal concept of liberty promised to individuals. It would not be possible to put women back into the model, since, in answer to Okin's question (1980),[7] a consideration of women as individuals would entail a radical restructuring of the family and the protected domain which would destroy the foundations of neo-liberalism, as it is premised on a certain role for the family.

Neo-liberalism is questioning the respective roles of the state, the family and the market in the sphere of social reproduction – that is, who takes the burden of the reproduction of labour power and maintenance and control of the non-working population. Gough (1983) believes that the Chicago School wishes to move social reproduction away from a combination of all three, as presently found in most societies, and more squarely onto the shoulders of the family – that is, women – and the free market.

Thus the example of libertarian feminist ideas demonstrates that their concentration on women's *rights* within the free market could not bring any significant improvement in women's position. It is therefore necessary to challenge the whole framework of neo-liberalism, demonstrating that both the maintenance of capitalism and the oppression of women are essential to the model. In sum it could never provide every individual with the best chance of doing well. Neo-liberalism therefore shares features with the bulk of political theory; while it appears genderless, it includes fundamental assumptions about women and their place in society which embody much of what feminism is trying to challenge both in its analysis and in its practice.

Notes

1. There are, however, two strands visible within the popularized versions such as 'Thatcherism': neo-liberalism, and authoritarianism or 'authoritarian populism'. These are not necessarily complementary. This chapter concentrates on the roots of the neo-liberal strand (see Hall and Jacques, eds, 1983; Levitas, 1985).

2. Friedman does this generally from the point of view of objective criteria such as higher average income, and Hayek generally from the perspective of absolute values. Both contain a value judgement, which is acceptable from Hayek given his methodology, but not so from Friedman.

3. Indeed for Hayek (1960, 1973) the form of government to provide this background of rules of just conduct does not by definition have to be democratic, as Friedman implies in his descriptions of the role of government. Liberalism and democracy, although compatible, are not the same, so a democratic government may be totalitarian and an authoritarian government may act on liberal principles; hence Hayek's distinction between authoritarianism and totalitarianism. Friedman (1976) believes that the danger with democracy is that voting becomes weighted in favour of special interests – therefore it is the economic market rather than the political one in which you get 'what you vote for'.

4. For Hayek, trade unions exercise coercion over other workers. The danger of unions is that they produce wage rigidities and uniformities. Trade unions should submit to the same principles of law as everybody else; for example, there is no reason why the right to strike should be an inalienable right.

5. There has not been much theoretical attention to these issues of liberalism by radical feminists. However there is one work (Cameron and Fraser, 1984) which deals with these issues by looking at the debate around a pornographic photograph in *The Guardian*.

6. Much of the literature on Chile during this period looks at the military regime very much in the context of their neo-liberal policies as a useful way to understand what happened. (See O'Brien, 1982, n.d.; Haworth and Roddick, n.d.; Foxley, 1982; for the effects on women see Prates, 1981; CHANGE, 1981.)

7. Okin (1980) asks what would happen to various models if women were included in them as individuals.

References

Barnes, Judy (n.d.) *The Case for Women's Rights*. Society for Libertarian Life.

Barrett, Michele (1981) *Women's Oppression Today*. London: Verso.

Barrett, Michele and Mary MacIntosh (1982) *The Anti-Social Family*. London: Verso.

Beechey, Veronica (1979) 'On Patriarchy', *Feminist Review*, 3: 66–82.

Brittan, Samuel (1980) 'Hayek, the New Right and the Crisis of Social Democracy', *Encounter*, 54(1): 31–46.

Cameron, Debbie and Liz Fraser (1984) 'The Liberal Organ: Needs, Rights and Pornography in the *Guardian*', *Trouble and Strife*, 4: 23–7.

CHANGE (1981) *Military Ideology and the Dissolution of Democracy. Women In Chile*. London: CHANGE International Reports.

Edholm, Felicity, Olivia Harris and Kate Young (1977) 'Conceptualizing Women', *Critique of Anthropology*, 9/10: 101–30.

Foxley, Alexandro (1982) 'Towards a Free Market Economy: Chile 1974–1979', *Journal of Development Economics*, 10(1): 1–29.

Friedman, Milton (1953) *Essays in Positive Economics*. Chicago: University of Chicago Press.

Friedman, Milton (1962) *Capitalism and Freedom*. Chicago: University of Chicago Press.

Friedman, Milton (1976) 'The Line We Dare Not Cross: the Fragility of Freedom', *Encounter*, 47(11): 8–15.

Gamble, Andrew (1979) 'The Free Economy and the Strong State: the Rise of the Social Market Economy', *Socialist Register*, 1–25.

Gough, Ian (1983) 'Thatcherism and the Welfare State', pp. 148–68 in S. Hall and M. Jacques (eds), *The Politics of Thatcherism*. London: Lawrence & Wishart.

Hall, Stuart and Martin Jacques (eds) (1983) *The Politics of Thatcherism*. London: Lawrence & Wishart.

Hartmann, Heidi (1981) 'The Unhappy Marriage of Marxism and Feminism', pp. 1–41 in L. Sargent (ed.), *Women and Revolution: A Discussion of the Unhappy Marriage of Marxism and Feminism*. London: Pluto.

Haworth, Nigel and Jackie Roddick (n.d.) 'Chile 1924 and 1979: Labour Policy and Industrial Relations through Two Revolutions'. Unpublished mimeo. University of Glasgow.

Hayek, Friedrich A. von (1945) *Individualism True and False*. Dublin: 12th Finlay Lecture, University College.

Hayek, Friedrich A. von (1960) *The Constitution of Liberty*. London: Routledge.

Hayek, Friedrich A. von (1967a) 'The Economy, Science and Politics', pp. 251–69 in F.A. Hayek, *Studies in Philosophy, Politics and Economics*. London: Routledge.

Hayek, Friedrich A. von (1967b) 'Theory of Complex Phenomena', pp. 22–42 in F.A. Hayek, *Studies in Philosophy, Politics and Economics*. London: Routledge.

Hayek, Friedrich A. von (1967c) 'Principles of a Liberal Social Order', pp. 160–77 in F.A. Hayek, *Studies in Philosophy, Politics and Economics*. London: Routledge.

Hayek, Friedrich A. von (1973) *Economic Freedom and Representative Government*. London: IEA. Occasional Paper number 39.

Hayek, Friedrich A. von (1979) *Law, Legislation and Liberty*. Volume 1: *Rules and Order*. London: Routledge.

Jaggar, Alison (1983) *Feminist Politics and Human Nature*. Brighton: Harvester.

Kuhn, Annette and Anne Marie Wolpe (1978) *Feminism and Materialism*. London: Routledge.

Levitas, Ruth (1985) 'New Right Utopias', *Radical Philosophy*, 39: 3–9.

Mount, Ferdinand (1982) *The Subversive Family*. London: Jonathan Cape.

O'Brien, Philip (1982) *The New Leviathan: The Chicago School and the Chilean Regime 1973–80*. Glasgow: University of Glasgow Institute of Latin American Studies. Occasional Paper number 38.

O'Brien, Philip (n.d.) 'Old Wine for New Bottles: the Monetarist Experiment in Chile and Britain'. Unpublished mimeo. University of Glasgow.

Okin, Susan Moller (1980) *Women in Western Political Thought*. London: Virago.

Prates, Suzanna (1981) 'Women's Labour and Family Survival Strategies under "The Stabilisation Models" in Latin America'. Unpublished mimeo. IDS, University of Sussex.

IV

FEMINISM WITHIN THE DISCIPLINE OF POLITICAL SCIENCE

6
Feminist theory and political analysis

Judith Evans

Preface

This chapter arose from a concern that feminists had no adequate concept of politics. It appeared that either they did not see that the concept might be problematic, or their attempts to define it lacked theoretical rigour.

Searching the literature for signs that I was wrong served, in general, only to strengthen my belief. However, I came to the conclusion – the main argument of this chapter – that feminism had made a strong case for the abolition of the distinction characteristically made by political scientists between the public and private realms. (Such abolition would call for a far wider definition of politics, and of legitimate political action, than would currently be accepted by most students of politics.) Another conclusion, and my main secondary argument, is that without radical changes in its assumptions, liberalism is unable to further the feminist cause save in a very limited sense.

The chapter also proposes an answer to a question very plainly posed by the literature (or to be more exact, by its absence): why feminist political scientists have had so minimal an impact on the basic concepts of political science. It is here proposed that sociological factors such as the small proportion of political scientists who are women, and the possibly related downgrading of the study of women, have inhibited a radical challenge to the profession from within.

The accounts given here of liberal, radical and Marxist feminism are of necessity of a somewhat rudimentary character; and I have concentrated on those aspects of each school of thought that most directly concern my argument. The reference list will direct readers to works which give more detailed analyses of feminist thought.

In the fifteen to twenty years since second-wave feminism began, much has been contributed to various academic disciplines by adherents of the movement. It is doubtful, though, whether the nature and practice of those disciplines has greatly changed. What is sure is that the study of politics has altered very little. We know more now about how women vote, about their depiction in classic works of political thought, and about their virtual absence from the upper echelons of government. However, work on these topics has followed very conventional lines of inquiry. This in itself is not surprising. What is, perhaps, is that the movement appears to have made little or no impression on political theorizing; and to be more precise, on the various concepts of politics and the polity that political scientists hold.

What is proposed here, however, is not that feminists have produced nothing that could alter the study of politics. Rather, it is argued that if non-academic thought, and writings from other disciplines, are taken into account, it can be said that a major though not, as yet, successful challenge has been mounted to a key assumption of political science: the distinction, commonly thought of as liberal, between the public and the private realms.

One caveat concerning usage of the dichotomy must immediately be lodged. It is clear from the most recent major work on the topic (Benn and Gaus, eds, 1983) that even in purely theoretical terms, the public/private boundary is uncertain and shifting. For my present purposes, however, the initial and general position to be taken is that the family and analogous groupings constitute the putative private realm, and all else, the public. In arguing that if we accept the premises of feminism then we must abandon the distinction between the realms, I shall discuss, in turn, three major feminist schools of thought.[1]

The first feminist view to be discussed is liberal. It is not the view of the National Organization for Women, or the 300 Group, albeit it has certain affinities with them. It is perhaps best described, *pace* Spiro Agnew, as radical-liberal. While its adherents wish for a change beyond that of the granting of equal rights for women in employment, education, and so on, they essentially wish to make politically pluralist societies live up to their ideals, and believe that they can do so without massive social and political restructuring. Further, the means they would use to bring about change are, primarily, educational.

To understand this form of feminism and, indeed, the other tendencies I shall discuss, it is necessary to place them in the context of their origins: that is, of the genesis of second-wave feminism in general.[2]

In the late 1960s, women's liberation groups were formed in the US, the UK and Germany.[3] In the US, disillusionment with the civil rights and anti-war movements, and with Students for a Democratic Society and its successors, led women to form their own, 'consciousness-raising' groups: to show individuals that they were not alone, and to analyse and understand what will here be termed women's oppression. In the UK, students and others formed similar groups, largely in response to the elitism, sexism and sexual harassment rife within student socialist societies,[4] and the male-dominated left in general; though when a group was set up from outside the existing left associations, female socialists were frequently wary of the enterprise, and occasionally hostile to it. In Germany, the same disillusion was felt. However, the movement, always weaker than those of the US and UK, very rapidly became confined to 'life-style' politics, expressed in the establishment of women-only communes as opposed to the mixed communes from which the secession had come.

This, then, was the context within which the feminist critique of politics emerged and grew. Its early version is, as has been said, to be regarded as of liberal persuasion. (To call it the 'early' version is not, as will become clear, to say that it does not exist today.)

The critique, encapsulated in the now famous slogan 'the personal is political',[5] was in its initial formulation two-fold. Firstly, a woman's problems and discontents did not spring from her inadequacies, nor were they unique. They were shared with other women, and were caused by societal factors inimical to female happiness and fulfil-ment. Thus, it was said, they were political. Secondly, individual relationships with men were unequal: while a woman who challenged the dictates of gender stood alone, a man's views and practices were supported by other men, and by society in general.[6] Thus, again, personal relationships were political; hence the early 1970s' emphasis on sexuality, the sudden triumphant emergence and widespread acceptance of radical feminism[7] and political separatism, and – though to a lesser extent, and uneasily – of personal separatism and lesbianism.

This two-fold belief was the product of a stage in the women's movement when all (feminist) views were held to be equal, and all feminists, at least potentially, equally capable of articulating them. The intentions of these tenets were laudable, and their results often encouraging; had this not been so, they would still have constituted an intelligible reaction to the elitism and harassment practised by political men. However, their corollary was that there could be no leaders, spokespersons or privileged analysts, and that theoretical comment could easily be construed as personal attack. The movement at this stage, then, proceeded by a rather odd kind of theoretical practice: women sitting around agreeing with one another, encouraging the participation of the least articulate and most shy, while keeping a wary eye on any potential 'stars'. The aid these groups gave to many women, and their role in building a sisterhood both within and outside them, cannot be overestimated; but neither can it be ignored that they could hardly be expected to become forcing grounds for theoretical innovation. This was, of course, only one of the factors militating against the development of fully-fledged feminist theories; but it is here adjudged to have been a major one.

Before assessing the critique, it is important to say what it does not, or at that time did not, mean. Isolated writings to the contrary, it did not define the personal as political because of welfare state intervention in family life, nor was it related to tendencies in Marxist thought which saw the family in its socializing role as part of the ideological apparatus of the state. Its starting point was far more intimate. As Boals was later to point out,

> This is what is meant, for example, when Adrienne Rich speaks . . . of women's obsession with romantic love and the suffering it entails and calls for recognition that 'this way of grief is shared, unnecessary and political'. (Boals, 1975: 172)

The nature of this belief was doubtless related to the composition of the groups from whence it came: overwhelmingly white, middle class, well-educated, 'children' of the 1960s, and quite possibly casualties of the 'sexual revolution'. The groups were, that is, as Breines (1968: 145) said of the early- and middle-period US new left, uncovering 'the politics of their own unhappiness', from their relatively privileged perspective; ignoring broader economic and social concerns. This does not, though, invalidate the most important aspect of this perspective: that in embryo, it is a far more radical challenge to the public/private split than many later and more developed accounts. Here we have the notion that not merely the hurly-burly of the chaise longue, but also the settled peace of the marriage bed, are no private places, but the battleground of a divided society. Further, neither is the division equal, nor the battle fair. One side possesses the normative, physical and material clout, and that side is male.

The points raised by this view will later be discussed more fully. However, there are certain problems that call for immediate comment. Firstly, the meaning of 'politics' is not scrutinized. Clearly, there is a latent meaning of politics as comprising a basic ordering of social arrangements, including the definition of gender roles and their maintenance; and as being power-laden and potentially conflictual. However, it could be said that it is simply assumed that the collective and the political are the same phenomenon. Secondly, the nature and status of male dominance, and of its relation to society as a whole, are not adequately considered. To be more precise, it is obviously thought that male power is systematic in the sense of being widespread, if not indeed ubiquitous; but it is not clear whether it is thought to be systematic in the sense of being a necessary and integral part of the society and polity within which we live.[8] Thirdly, 'power' as a concept is taken for granted: it is something that men possess, by means of which they dominate women. Further than this, by their very nature, consciousness-raising groups were unlikely to go.

Beliefs similar to those of the critique are expressed more fully, albeit in a rather different form, by the radical pluralist Iglitzin. Her first salvo (1972a) consists of an argument to the effect that girls and women have been, and are, repressively socialized to remain within the private realm; and they are taught the supposed virtues concomitant with that seclusion, and antithetical to successful forays outside its bounds. Meanwhile, they also learn, courtesy of the tenets of pluralism, that politics is open to all; and thus that if they renounce the political world, it is by their own free choice. Well might a hypothesized ruling class or power elite envy so devilish a form of indoctrination. But does it exist? If so, does it work? Who is responsible for it? – and whose interests does it serve? Liberal feminism only really attempts to answer the first two of these questions.

Good mainstream political scientist that she is, Iglitzin seeks to test her assumptions by two political socialization studies: one of the most conventional kind, and a second investigating gender socialization, and its relation to political learning (1972b). The hypotheses, as we might expect, are that girls will score less well than boys on political tests, and be heavily sex-stereotyped; and that the two sets of attributes will be correlated. Briefly, given the data, the safest verdict on Iglitzin's case is 'not proven', though there is evidence that, for some girls, domestic life overshadows all other endeavours (1972b: 12). However, Iglitzin does not try to use this finding to rescue her argument, nor does she simply say that she was wrong. Rather, she casts doubt on the validity of all extant political socialization research, hers included, suggesting that sexist phrasing, and the use of an outmoded concept of politics, have biased results (1972b: 19f.). More specifically, a focus on institutions and their incumbents has precluded investigations of a broader field of political endeavour, and of informal relations of power. *A fortiori*, all such studies have seriously devalued the potential of women and girls, by ignoring the very areas to which their attention is directed. Research should therefore concentrate on micro-level politics: on, for example, family interaction and power within the home, the peer group and school, and on issues such as soft drugs, Vietnam, the conscription of women, and bussing.

> And in this sense perhaps girls, who traditionally score low on the old-style questions . . . are really smarter than boys!

> Maybe girls will prove to be more sensitive to power relationships in home and family. If [they] do at least as well . . . [the research] will have been worth doing to lay to rest the tired old myths . . . about women's abilities. But beyond such strictly feminist concerns, such a study will be worth-while if it serves to personalize politics, to enlighten people by showing them that politics is everywhere . . . and thus that no-one is apolitical. (1972b: 23–4)

Again, 'politics is everywhere' relates neither to the pervasive character of the state, nor to the scope of the ideological hegemony of a ruling group. The concept is of politics as power-based interaction; and an interaction that is, in effect, everywhere the same. However, the conduct of politics is not immutable. The attributes that accrue to women by reason of their servitude could, unleashed, transform the mores of the polity:

> . . . perhaps with new values and goals in our educational system men, too, can become loving and gentle in their political relationships . . . Such an education may well encourage introspection and subjectivity, a joining of the private and the public spheres . . . (1972a: 254)

Various problems are raised by Iglitzin's account. Firstly, while it is clear that she would distinguish between micro- and macro-politics, it is not obvious where she thinks the demarcation line should be drawn. Secondly, although, as I have suggested, it appears that politics as power-play is everywhere the same, still – given the supposed attributes of women – it might be inferred that different styles of political behaviour predominate at the different levels; but this we are not told. Thirdly, while it must be noted that Iglitzin qualifies her hopes for a more feminine political future, this does not prevent us from questioning its realism. The polity might indeed be transformed by an influx of female values; but it seems eminently more likely that women, reassured of their worth, will be glad to retreat to their customary habitat. Heads, men win; tails, women lose. After all, politics is everywhere, and everyone is political.

This last formulation must also be probed, for the ubiquity of politics should not be equated with the politicization of all. If we are to consider micro-politics as consisting of the formal decision-making processes most proximate to a citizen's daily life, that does not entail even a supposition that all persons participate in them, let alone that all have equal power over the outcome. If on the contrary micro-politics is politicking – that is, engaging in power-based interaction, in this case outside the formal political arena – then while all are presumably in some way involved, it is unlikely that all are equally skilled. Indeed – and perhaps not surprisingly, given that politicking as here defined occurs in both the public and private realms – there is some evidence that men are better manipulators than women (*Annual Review of Anthropology*, 1977: 195). While it is not, then, totally implausible to suggest that women are more aware of power within the family, it is illegitimate extrapolation to say that for that reason they are the more political sex. To be political, it is, on the whole, necessary to act politically. Yet of course we see women dominated within the family; and outside it, beyond the most basic and conventional citizen level, their political participation is curtailed by socialization, male retaliation, and the pragmatic demands of their current familial role. In the words of Kirkpatrick,

> A woman who becomes an engineer not only does not gain points on the male status ladder . . . or on the female hierarchy, she can lose points for inappropriate behavior . . . A woman entering politics risks the social and psychological penalties so frequently associated with nonconformity. Disdain, internal conflicts, and failure are widely believed to be her likely rewards. (1974: 15)

Liberal theory has either approved this situation, or not sought to encompass it. The question remaining is whether it can do so, and yet be liberal.

It does not seem unreasonable to suggest that the genuinely liberal liberal theorist, if such a term be permitted, is here faced with something of a Gordian knot. On the one hand, liberalism is dedicated to personal autonomy and individual liberty, and the state may intervene to ensure their maintenance. Nevertheless, this raises the questions of whether all should have the same range of choices, of how family and state socialization are to relate to one another, and of how legitimate the latter is. However, these matters can presumably be resolved, if only in theory. On the other hand, liberalism is also dedicated to the separation of the public realm of political action and impersonal social interaction, and the private realm of conjoined individuals; the area where, free from the demands of all but those with whom they choose to associate, people can recuperate, repro-duce, rest, and play. Paradigmatically, as Benn and Gaus (eds, 1983: 38) have said, this realm is the family.

Now historically, in fact and in the writings of liberal theorists, and in fact, in very large part, today, women are the servitors of the private realm. It is not, for them, a retreat from the public spaces of life. Rather, either they are not public persons except in the most minimal sense, or their place in both realms simply imposes two sets of burdens upon them. To paraphrase Denning, MR, in *Wachtel v Wachtel* (1973) – a landmark apportionment case following the Divorce Law Reform Act of 1969 – the former husband will incur the added expense of hiring a housekeeper, while his ex-wife, whether or not she works outside the home, will expect to perform that task herself. Within marriage, of course, a woman also bears and rears children, cares for her husband's sexual[9] and sartorial well-being and self-respect, shops and cooks, and performs other functions thought proper to her sex. In effect, the public realm is parasitic on the efforts of half the adult inhabitants of the private. Pateman (1983: 281f., passim) has well characterized this state of affairs as patriarchal-liberalism; the question remains whether sexual parity can be attained without the collapse of the family.

Currently, of course, and despite non-interventionist rhetoric from certain quarters, the private realm is certainly not immune from the attentions of the mixed-economy, liberal welfare state. Indeed, personal relationships of the most intimate kind are subject to legal scrutiny. Legislation following the Wolfenden Report laid down very precisely indeed the conditions under which male homosexual activity could occur; lesbian mothers have frequently, on the sole ground of their sexual preference, been deprived of their children on divorce; and – though enforcement of this law depends very much on the circumstances – an age of consent is given for heterosexual intercourse. Further, the family itself is subject to state intervention, in at least four ways. Firstly, there are welfare benefits designed to help the family maintain a reasonable standard of living, and thus keep the family unit intact. Secondly, children may be taken into care if it is thought that such action is conducive to their welfare (though it should be noted that comparative social deprivation leading to an impoverishment of life chances and choices is not a ground for such action), and it appears all too easy for this separation to be made permanent, against the parents' wishes. Thirdly, the state as personified by the police is most reluctant to intrude in cases of 'domestics', that is, where it is a matter of a husband using violence against his wife. There may well be prudential reasons for this: but the probable major reason, and the certain effect, is to reinforce the existence and mores of the patriarchal family. (This category is termed intervention because it involves non-neutrality by an agent of the state, a decision to treat certain kinds of behaviour differently, according to their context.) Fourthly, the state does not treat the family consistently, but according to the economic and political conditions of the time. To take the most obvious case, in time of war women are expected to undertake paid employment, and communal facilities are provided to ease the burden of the double shift; while in peace time, the ideology of the privatized family is renewed. Less obviously, for some time now, but certainly related to the onset of economic recession, the major political parties have reaffirmed the importance of the family. There have been the usual murmurings about the injustice of married women obtaining an 'extra' income, the effects on children of a lack of mother-care, and other such commonplace sayings of our culture. Further, while plans to shift the treatment of certain categories of long-term patients from psychiatric hospitals to 'the community' are supposed to be accompanied by an increase in the relevant official local caring services, it does not require a commitment to conspiracy theory to assume that the main burden of this in essence most enlightened policy will fall on the state's favourite flexible resource – women.

In our society, then, the privacy of the private realm is a somewhat artificial one. Privacy of conforming individuals within that realm there is; but at a very high price for women. The question to be pursued is whether it is possible for interventionist measures that could be accepted by liberals – basically, laws or practices that would affect the private realm only indirectly – to bring about sexual equality. Such measures would be educational when they touched on matters such as the division of domestic labour, but coercive when they concerned such matters as education, employment, and remun-eration. (I am assuming that they would also be more radical, and more effective, than current equal opportunity legislation.) A massive extension of part-time work, not poorly paid and of low prestige, and not primarily the preserve of women, would seem also to be necessary; though more flexible working hours, and more autonomy within work, could act as a substitute. Then perhaps liberalism could maintain its private realm, and with rather less tension than exists at present.

Before this blithe and eminently liberal conclusion can be accepted, though, the very early formulation of 'the personal is polit-ical' must be revisited. If that *cri de coeur* indeed concerns the anguish of the heart, and if, as O'Brien (1981: 210) suggests, the aim is that '. . . men and women abandon their long preoccupation with sleeping together in favour of being awake together', then it would seem that the search is to transcend the modal male–female relation-ship, where the man is or is in some way deemed to be in some way superior to the woman, and establish a more androgynous society. Now liberalism can countenance socialization to the point where the individual can reject it: can, that is, accept learning rather than inter-nalization.[10] What, then, of the deviants, in the proposed new order?

What, to use the crudest analogy possible, of the resolute Tarzan and Jane, who choose these roles despite what they have been taught, and whatever options may have been presented to them? They might dutifully attempt to socialize their children towards the new ways, and yet, so subtle is parent–child interaction, influence them towards the old. Others, too, might follow. The attaining of sexual equality might thus be subverted by the unwillingness of liberalism – and this is of course an old liberal dilemma – to restrict the freedom of speech and expression save where they amount to an incitement to harm (harm here virtually amounting to physical danger, or severe economic deprivation). Thus a liberal value of equality of opportunity would be voided by the liberal ideal of tolerance. Here one critic (not directly concerned with feminism) argues for:

> . . . a notion of truth that resists mindless tolerance; all ideas are not equally true, and hence not all are equally tolerable . . . The free market of ideas has never been free, but always a market. To undo this requires not commissars and censors but critical intelligence loyal to an objective notion of truth. If there is repressive tolerance, there is also liberating intolerance. (Jacoby, 1977: xviii)

As I have said, the liberal unwillingness to accept such a viewpoint places in jeopardy the feminist project. It raises the question of whether a feminist can, in all conscience, remain a liberal. Many have, though for varied reasons, chosen other ways.

At some stage or another, many women have felt that radical feminism held the key to their discontent. In the initial stages of the movement, this may well have been attributable to the skill and perception of Firestone's (1971) chapters on love and romance,[11] and to the simplicity of the early radical feminist analysis. However, its appeal may also have sprung from its adherents' political activity. Where liberal angels and Marxist cadres have hesitated to tread, radical feminists have marched. While inadequate thought on the reasons for action, and the location of targets, have undoubtedly posed problems for the remainder of the movement, radical feminism has alerted us to many wrongs. Moreover, it is a virtue that, by its very existence, it keeps the issue of the politics of sexuality and sexual preference alive.

Briefly, radical feminism postulates classification by sex as the earliest and most important division in society; espouses separatism, both political and personal; and is more closely associated with lesbianism than any other feminist grouping.[12] Its revolution consists in repossessing control over the means of biological reproduction, though thereafter the vision varies, along a continuum from Firestone's remarkably prescient 'test-tube baby' ideal to the recognition and celebration of 'natural' maternity.

Various other issues, too, are raised and discussed by radical feminism. However, both within the movement and in academic circles it is best known for its use of the concept of patriarchy, which has been and continues to be the locus of a fierce debate with Marxist feminists. This is not the patriarchy of Filmer; or of any other writer, antecedent to the movement, who has employed the term. It is well defined by O'Brien:

> Paterfamilias, to preserve his freedom, requires family law, fraternal co-operation and ideological legitimation. He also, then as now, retained the option of brutality to enforce his domestic power. *Far from being a paradigm of political power or the social precondition of public renown, patriarchy and the doctrine of potency are the products of political power, the creation of a brotherhood of fathers acting collectively to implement their definition of manhood in social and ideological forms.* (1981: 103–4)

It is easy to see that acceptance of the concept of patriarchy leads to rejection of the reality of the public/private split, and an appreciation of its strength as an ideological construct. Again to quote O'Brien,

> Only under intense social upheaval does the strength of the abstract wall between public and private tremble, and its fetishistic nature stand exposed as male invention. (1981: 114)

The notion of patriarchy, as has been said, has been forcefully attacked by Marxist feminists. Briefly, they cannot accept the sex division as more important than that of class; and they regard the concept of patriarchy as employed by radical feminists as static, ahistorical, and incapable of accounting for vast cultural variation in the way male dominance is expressed. (This point could of course be accepted without jettisoning the concept, if 'patriarchy' were to be understood as an ideal type.) The criticism to be made here is rather different. The concept of patriarchy offers neither a clearly articulated definition of politics, nor an explanation, as opposed to a description, of the condition of women. (This point is not identical with the 'ahistorical' charge made by Marxist feminists.) Why should state socialism, or capitalism, need to rely on the subordination of women? What is added to our understanding of society, if we say that it is run by men?

Insofar as there is a radical feminist answer to the second question, it is that rule by men is despotic and cruel, and relies, in the end, on brute force. After the radical feminist revolution, men would accept female values: love, compassion, kindliness. The lust for power would disappear with the power of lust.

A view similar to this is held by many women who are not radical feminists; I have discussed it at length elsewhere (Evans, 1984). Here it should be said simply that, firstly, there is inadequate proof that men and women differ in the way suggested. Secondly, even if the postulated attributes did exist, if they were the products of socialization, then the transformation of society might adversely affect them. If on the other hand they were biologically based, only a matriarchal revolution, and female rule, could bring about the kind of society that radical feminists would wish to see. Quite apart from the fact that – popular views to the contrary notwithstanding – such asymmetry is not the radical feminist utopia, how could a matriarchy succeed, against the proclivities and might of men, in establishing and maintaining itself?

The conclusion must be, then, that again the basic contribution of radical feminism lies in its attack on the split between the private and public realms; an attack more coherent than that of the liberals, as it articulates the political connections of the 'public' and 'private' more clearly. However, the concept of patriarchy, as given here, must be accepted at the very least as a heuristic device, before the latter statement can be adjudged to be true.

Marxist feminists are both helped and hindered by what radical feminism lacks: the presence of a clearly articulated theoretical framework within and against which to work. They are helped, because Marxism has placed the question of the oppression of women firmly on its agenda; hindered because of the behaviour of certain Marxist groupings, the insistence on the analytic primacy of class, and the manner in which the oppression of women was supposed to be overcome, which has rightly been perceived as inadequate. That is, the entry of women, in massive numbers, into the ranks of wage labour has not brought about sexual equality; though this statement should perhaps be qualified by an acceptance that there has not yet occurred a Marxist revolution of the type first envisaged, and that few Marxists, indeed, now defend state socialist societies. Nevertheless, this failure may explain why – despite the existence within Marxism of an analysis of the privatized family, counterposed to the public world of production, as a problem to be overcome – Marxist feminism has sought, as have other tendencies, to articulate and query the public/private dichotomy.

Given that the large-scale entry of women into the paid labour force has, if anything, worsened their lot, and further, given the view of many Marxists that feminist concerns are 'diversionary', it is not surprising that one form of attack on the conventions of Marxism has consisted in the assertion that women's reproductive role is as vital to the capitalist state as is production as it is normally understood. To quote Himmelweit and Mohun:

From the point of view of capital, housework is concerned with the reproduction of labour-power both on a daily and on a generational basis. (1977: 16)

Further, the family has a vital ideological role:

> . . . a crucial stabilising function through the allocation of sexually-defined roles, both in the conditioning of children and in the maintenance of a docile, disciplined and divided working class . . . Authoritarian relationships in social production (capitalist to worker) are facilitated through their previous observation and acceptance in the home (parents to children and husband to wife). (1977: 16)

The authors point out that Marxists have only begun the investigation, stemming from Marx, of 'soaring divorce rates, declining birth-rates and unprecedented involvement of the state in reproduction . . .'. They add:

> Given the current forces of production, two sexes are needed for reproduction. But this is not an explanation of why a sexual division of labour should have extended to include as women's work the education and care of the young, the old and the sick, and the replenishment of the living individual. *The division of productions between a public and a domestic sphere requires explanation in terms which do not take the sexual division of labour as an eternal constant.* (1977: 29)

This passage is of particular importance given its context: a critical review of the domestic labour debate. While the division between the public and domestic sphere appears not to be challenged,[13] the nature of the domestic realm is attacked in no uncertain terms. Further, while the public sector here is not the same as the public realm of the liberal theorist, empirically, if not ideologically, the domestic sphere is very close indeed to the private.

In one version of Marxism, the family is of course only partially privatized; for in its socializing role, it is viewed as an 'ideological state apparatus' (ISA) maintaining the hegemony of the ruling class, or alternatively, of the capitalist world-view. However, various feminists, including Coward and Ellis (1977: 73)[14] have argued that, depending on one's concept of ideology, the family may properly be seen not as an ISA, but as a far more autonomous entity: thus opening up the possibility of feminist struggle within it, but with implications beyond its boundaries. There might be thought to be a certain irony here, in that feminists are attacking a tendency of thought that denies, to an extent, the reality of the public/private split even under capitalism; but the point, in this theoretical context, is that the tendency has to be attacked, if feminist action is to be considered possible.

Thus it may be said again, albeit more tentatively, and with due recognition of the fact that Marxism has always sought to remove women from the domestic realm (though in practice, women's liberation is either an issue to be used in pursuit of rather different goals, or something to be achieved 'after the revolution'), that the major contribution of Marxist feminism to political theory lies in its onslaught on the public/private distinction. As has already been suggested in the discussion of liberalism, it is difficult to envisage great changes in the private realm, without the virtual abolition of the split.

Of the feminist writers quoted or cited here, only two are political scientists. What, then, are the reasons for the apparent inability of feminist political scientists in the US and UK even to attempt to challenge the basic tenets of their discipline? It cannot be, as has been suggested of non-academic feminism, that female political scientists abhor politics and power, and thus evade their investigation. It may be that we have internalized disciplinary norms, including epistemological tenets, that preclude a successful feminist challenge to political science: with Nietzsche, though for different reasons, we are entrapped in a bottle from which the flies will not escape (Strong, 1982: 174). This I do not believe. In any event, it seems unnecessary to resort to such explanations when there are obvious sociological factors, and clearly prior ones, which inhibit the development of liberatory feminist thought within the discipline.

The first factor considered relevant, though more applicable to the UK than the US, is the small proportion and therefore the small number of political scientists who are women. Not all the women will be feminists (though a surprising number are); among the feminists, not all will be working on topics related to women; and in the 'women and politics' field, most researchers will probably be engaged in study, be it theoretical or empirical, which indeed adds to our knowledge, but has no immediately obvious chance of changing our perception of politics.

Secondly, in both the US and the UK, and despite the 'women's studies' publishing boom, the study of women and politics is not, from a purely self-interested point of view, the best enterprise with which to be associated. In the UK, it is true, token feminist chapters appear in books on, for example, democratic theory; thus neatly trapping those who want or need publications, or who feel that the message is ultimately more important than the medium, but who nevertheless dislike tokenism. In the US, there is more of a career path, with female patronage; but it is still preferable to be a political scientist who happens to write about women, rather than a member of a department of, or centre for, women's studies. In the former case, too, it helps to have made one's name in a different area, prior to undertaking research on women.

These problems have a further implication: that those who choose to study women will strive to be, vis-a-vis the discipline, like Caesar's wife; making it even less likely that their work will be path-breaking. It is at least possible that these factors explain why, as Pateman has said,

> The feminist total critique of the liberal opposition of public and private still awaits its philosopher. (1983: 300)

Notes

1. There are, of course, more than three strands within contemporary feminism. There exist, for example, eco-feminism and anarcho-feminism; and revolutionary feminism, which is part of the radical school. The most obvious omission from my text is socialist feminism; in this specific context, my view is that, composed as it is of aspects of radical and Marxist feminism, it adds to the discussion exactly what they add.

2. Contemporary feminism has been dated from the publication of Friedan (1963). However, the groupings I discuss seem to have appeared later than, and not as a consequence of, this fruitful work (Freeman, 1975).

3. Differing accounts of the initial stages of the movement in the UK are given here, in Coote and Campbell (1982), and by Rowbotham (1983). Lacking sufficient documentation, the various authors have relied to an extent on their own experiences and perceptions.

4. It was a leading member of the London School of Economics Socialist Society who in 1969 paraphrased the then Stokely Carmichael thus: 'The place of a woman in the revolution is prone'.

5. It could of course be argued that the slogan derives from early and middle period US New Left thought.

6. Obviously a deviant man would face similar difficulties; but at that time, generally speaking, male homosexuals had not 'come out'.

7. A transient acceptance, for many; but one that left its mark.

8. I am grateful to Albert Weale for articulating this point.

9. 'In two of these cases the woman had been found guilty of cruelty by refusing to have intercourse even though in one of them her refusal was due entirely to an invincible fear of conception and childbirth. In the other two the husband (apparently undersexed and innately disinclined to have intercourse) had been found not guilty of cruelty even though this resulted in intercourse at rare intervals and in one case in total abstinence for fifteen years. The inference to be drawn is that the courts are demanding different standards of sexual participation from husbands and wives' (Bromley, 1977: 189–90).

10. I am grateful to John Robinson for discussing this point.

11. I speak of the UK; it appears that in the US Millett (1972) was more influential.

12. This is not, of course, to say that all radical feminists are lesbians, or all lesbians, radical feminists.

13. This is, of course, because the authors are concerned to a certain extent simply to analyse capitalism as it exists, rather than to offer prescriptions for a better society.

14. I am indebted to Alex Callinicos for directing me to this source.

References

Annual Review of Anthropology. (1977).

Ardener, S. (ed.) (1981) *Perceiving Women.* London: Dent.

Balbus, I. (1982) *Marxism and Domination.* Princeton: Princeton University Press.

Barrett, M. (1980) *Women's Oppression Today.* London: Verso.

Benn, S. and S. Gaus (eds) (1983) *Public and Private in Social Life.* London: Croom Helm.

Boals, K. (1975) 'Review: Political Science', *Signs*, I(1): 161–74.

Bouchier, D. (1983) *The Feminist Challenge.* London: Macmillan.

Bowles, G. and R. Klein (eds) (1983) *Theories of Women's Studies.* London: Routledge.

Breines, P. (1968) 'Marxism and the New Left in America', pp. 133–51 in J. Habermas (ed.), *Antworten auf Herbert Marcuse.* Frankfurt: Suhrkump Verlag.

Bromley, P. (1977) *Family Law.* London: Butterworth.

Coote, A. and B. Campbell (1982) *Sweet Freedom.* Oxford: Blackwell.

Coward, R. (1983) *Patriarchal Precedents.* London: Routledge.

Coward, R. and J. Ellis (1977) *Language and Materialism.* London: Routledge.

Dreitzel, H. (ed.) (1972) *Family, Marriage and the Struggle of the Sexes.* London: Macmillan.

Duncan, G. (ed.) (1983) *Democratic Theory and Practice.* Cambridge: Cambridge University Press.

Ehrenreich, B. (1983) *The Hearts of Men.* London: Pluto.

Eisenstein, Z. (ed.) (1979) *Capitalist Patriarchy and the Case for Socialist Feminism.* New York and London: Monthly Review Press.

Elshtain, J. (1981) *Public Man, Private Woman.* Oxford: Martin Robertson.

Elshtain, J. (ed.) (1982) *The Family in Political Thought.* Brighton: Harvester.

Evans, Judith. (1984) 'The Good Society? Implications of a Greater Participation by Women in Public Life', *Political Studies*, XXXII (4): 618–26.

Firestone, S. (1971) *The Dialectic of Sex.* London: Jonathan Cape (first published 1970).

Freeman, J. (1975) *The Politics of Women's Liberation.* New York: David McKay.

Friedan, B. (1963) *The Feminist Mystique.* Harmondsworth: Penguin.

Friedman, S. and E. Sarah (eds) (1982) *On the Problem of Men.* London: The Women's Press.

Hartsock, N. (1983) *Money, Sex, and Power.* London: Longman.

Himmelweit, S. and S. Mohun (1977) 'Domestic Labour and Capital', *Cambridge Journal of Economics*, I(1): 15–31.

Iglitzin, L. (1972a) 'Political Education and Sexual Liberation', *Politics and Society*, II(2): 241–59.

Iglitzin, L. (1972b) 'Sex-Typing and Politicization in Children's Attitudes'. Paper presented to the Annual General Meeting of the American Political Science Association.

Jacoby, R. (1977) *Social Amnesia.* Brighton: Harvester.

Jaggar, A. (1983) *Feminist Politics and Human Nature.* Brighton: Harvester.

Janssen-Jurreit, M. (1982) *Sexism.* London: Pluto.

Kirkpatrick, J.J. (1974) *Political Woman.* New York: Basic Books.

McAllister, P. (ed.) (1982) *Reweaving the Web of Life.* Philadelphia: New Society Publishers.

Marks, E. (ed.) (1981) *New French Feminisms.* Brighton: Harvester.

Millett, K. (1972) *Sexual Politics.* London: Abacus.

Oakley, A. (1982) *Subject Women*. London: Fontana.

O'Brien, M. (1981) *The Politics of Reproduction*. London: Routledge.

Pateman, C. (1983) 'Feminist Critiques of the Public/Private Dichotomy', pp. 281–303 in S. Benn and S. Gaus (eds), *Public and Private in Social Life*. London: Croom Helm.

Reiter, R. (1975) *Toward an Anthropology of Women*. New York: Monthly Review Press.

Rowbotham, S. (1983) *Dreams and Dilemmas*. London: Virago.

Sanday, P. (1982) *Female Power and Male Dominance*. Cambridge: Cambridge University Press.

Sargent, L. (ed.) (1981) *The Unhappy Marriage of Marxism and Feminism*. London: Pluto.

Sayers, J. (1982) *Biological Politics*. London: Tavistock.

Spender, D. (ed.) (1983) *Feminist Theorists*. London: The Women's Press.

Stacey, M. and M. Price (1981) *Women, Power and Politics*. London: Tavistock.

Strong, T. (1982) 'Oedipus as Hero: Family and Family Metaphors in Nietzsche', pp. 173–96 in J. Elshtain (ed.), *The Family in Political Thought*. Brighton: Harvester.

Yates, G. (1977) *What Women Want*. Cambridge, MA and London: Harvard University Press.

Young, I. (1980) 'Socialist Feminism and the Limits of Dual Systems Theory', *Socialist Review*, 50–51, X (2/3): 169–88.

7
Women's studies and political studies

Elizabeth Meehan

Preface

'Political science has been the least affected by the impact of the new (feminist) ideas . . .' (Bonder, 1983: 570). 'Political science was one of the last social science areas to respond to the interest in women's roles triggered by "second-wave" feminism . . .' (Randall, 1983: 38).

My main conclusion in this chapter is that teaching about the politics of women probably must take place on two fronts: separately and in conventional courses on political institutions and theory. There is a line of argument which uses the precedent set by other 'breakaway' disciplines, including political science itself, to show that separation is the best way of integrating theories, traditions, methods and substantive knowledge into a unified whole. On the other hand, I suggest that we cannot allow male students to avoid questioning and evaluating their assumptions about women. It is primarily male assumptions which, for the present, inform policies that limit the lives of women. And, after all, we expect such critical analysis by students in all other spheres of enquiry.

In reaching this position, I have also concluded that, if political analysis and theory themselves are to be improved along lines that their mainly male practitioners appear to want, feminist theories are a prerequisite. The innovatory directions in the discipline which appear both to invite and to require a feminist perspective are those which seek to explain the informal processes that deprive other subordinate classes or groups of access to formal decision-making institutions. In particular, recent disputes about whether to abandon or to reconstruct the notion of the public sphere cannot be assessed or resolved without reference to feminist theories of politics.

But in developing a feminist political theory or theories, we cannot, in my view, do so wholly separately. Knowledge that takes us beyond tautologies cannot, as the classical rationalists would have wished, be acquired in a vacuum. We are dependent upon, as well as able to enrich, what is already known. It is as a result of stimulation by the positive elements of established theory as well as by explorations of its discrepancies and irrationalities that the construction of new theories takes place. It is also necessary to be eclectic in where we look for our insights. Feminism is about the whole lives of all women. It is not about a discrete aspect of the policy process which may affect part of the lives of some element of society – as might be, for example, the politics of a choice between building a motorway or a dual carriageway. Consequently, the sources on which we draw must be correspondingly broad; depending on aims, they may include literature, psychology and personal experience as well as the more obvious politics, economics, sociology and various branches of philosophy.

This chapter is not a review of the inadequacies of the political science literature on women. Reviews of work rectifying past omissions have been done already (Randall, 1983: Vallance, 1982).[1] It is intended, here, to try to push the criticisms quoted at the start back a stage and to deal with 'meta' level problems inherent in the inadequacies of the conventional literature. This leads to a paradox. That is, that political science above all disciplines, ought to lead rather than to lag, in dealing with questions about women's rights and roles. That it does not is particularly surprising in view of its explorations in the last twenty or thirty years into more informal political processes, into how issues are kept off political agenda and into more complex understanding of power relationships.

This problem is tackled first by discussing ideas in the philosophy and sociology of language which suggest that the concepts and categories we use to describe the world also serve to limit our understanding of it and, therefore, influence what can be regarded as possible social practice. The chapter then draws attention to links between specific parts of the previous discussion and the writing about and teaching of women's studies. These are the use of apparently simple forms of naming, the significance of historical knowledge and questions of disciplinary organization. Here it is argued that disciplinary divisions are themselves categorizations embodying the same difficulties as the categories used to denote specific, substantive objects of analysis. It is at this point that the disciplinary innovations referred to above become particularly relevant to the relationship between political studies and women's studies. The chapter then moves on to the future of that relationship, discussing various possible directions in literature and course organization. Finally, in view of the connections posited in the sociology of language between language and social practice, the chapter discusses the relationship between our methods of teaching and writing about women and forms of political organization and participation.

Language, power and ideology

The naming of objects may seem, on the face of it, a neutral process; objects are 'out there' and require symbols to denote them. But philosophers and linguists disagree. For Wittgenstein, 'language is the vehicle of thinking' (Brand, ed., 1979: 53–66). It can only function through 'understanding, intending, interpreting and thinking'. Things, whether apparently simple like toothache or complex like marriage, cannot be named intelligibly except by words which already carry meanings; and these meanings are not straightforward symbols, as in algebra, but embody complicated understandings of traditions, values and assumptions about appropriate behaviour. Language is necessarily social, determining how a society sees and thinks about reality and thus shapes its institutions.[2] Similar theories are proposed by sociologists of language. Goody and Watt (1963: 313) cite evidence to suggest that names are first given to phenomena that are connected with direct, pragmatic interests and not to peripheral or abstract things.[3] Primitive language, then, influences what generations of users regard as important; changes among peripheral phenomena would go unnoticed or unrecorded because there would be no way of describing them. Names, having been established, do not simply restrict the extent of knowledge. An objective need for names, in turn, sets up subjective frameworks of analysis which vary according to the choice of form of denotation. For example, Goody and Watt (1963: 313) also point out, that, in northern Ghana, days are reckoned according to markets; the very word for 'day' and 'market' is the same. The word 'day', then, denotes not a mathematical set of equal units of time, but a form of socioeconomic activity.

Although it is not always clear that there is agreement about the direction of causality, sociologists of language share Wittgenstein's view that there is a close connection between language, social ideas and social practice. Language is both an indicator and a cause of social change (Giglioli, ed., 1972: 309). Nowhere is this view clearer than when sociologists of language are talking about power relationships in society. Bernstein (1970: 158, 162–4, 167–70, 171–7) draws on Durkheim and Marx in arguing that there is a link between symbolic systems, social structures and the shaping of experience, changes in symbolic systems being governed by parental or class power. He argues that the language codes of working class children may allow them to show more imagination than the children of the middle class. The latter, however, are more easily able to cope with the system and rules of logic which determine what kind of knowledge is to be considered valid. Brown and Gilman (1960: 252–82) provide an illuminating case study of how names and the rules of their use reflect established power relationships, help to cause change and can be taken as indicators of more general ideological frameworks.

Their work is about the familiar and formal uses of the pronouns tu and vous, tu and vos, thee and you, etc. The use of the plural 'vos', seems to have arisen because there were once *two* Roman emperors; one for the east and one for the west. Each receiving 'vos' referred to himself as 'we'. The use of 'vos' continued, even when there was one emperor, not to denote plurality, but because the addressee was the emperor; it became a mark of deference to power. Furthermore, the nobility, also being powerful, used it to each other, reserving 'tu' to refer to inferiors, sometimes including wives and children as well as subordinate classes. Subordinates used 'tu' among themselves and 'vos' to superiors. This pattern, in turn, generated a sense of solidarity among those who addressed each other in similar fashion. More complicated patterns developed to accommodate solidaristic emotions that crossed class boundaries, distinctions being made, for example, in forms of address to personal servants and waiters. The use of 'tu' among French revolutionaries was a mark of solidarity and part of an effort to promote ideological and actual social change. Attempts to ban the use of 'vous' after the revolution were made both to denote an actual change of class relations and to reinforce the new social order. Similarly in England, the Quakers used 'thee' and 'thou' because they held egalitarian beliefs and to provoke others to use egalitarian forms and to think and behave accordingly. In modern surveys of young Europeans, Brown and Gilman show that individual choice of pronoun is a good predictor of more general ideologies about property, nationalization and power relationships in society. They also point out that societies which have remained most hierachical are also those with least change in pronoun usage; for example, societies in which Afrikaans, Gujarati and Hindi are spoken.

The arguments of Bernstein and of Brown and Gilman apply to oral and written language. Written language is important in another way. This is because of the views expressed by Goody and Watt (1963: 319–51) about the different ways in which senses of the past are related to thinking about the present. Oral traditions of communicating cultures transform history according to current social needs. In the past and present, history and myth intermingle. Written records provide what they call a more objective account of the past. This can give rise to disputes, especially when, as in Africa, they are set against ever-changing oral accounts. If in literate societies written records are 'objective', then they must become the 'authorized versions'. But, if Bernstein is right that knowledge is controlled by the conventions of the dominant class, then written records – as well as current oral usages – become a tool for the continuation of class power.

If most of the time most people are not aware that language is not neutral, in time of upheaval language does become politically contentious. I have already referred to the French revolutionaries. More recently, there has been administrative reassessment and grass-roots pressure about what to call racial minorities.[4] Social scientists ought always to be aware of the political implications of language use. The business of naming is no different from categorizing, making analytical distinctions, and finding symbols for them. These are the very purposes of the occupation; and the difficulty cannot be overcome in the use of abstract symbols because the object (or subject) of enquiry is qualitatively different for the social scientist compared to the mathematician.

The sociology of deviance and development studies are the two main social sciences in which practitioners have self-consciously tried to come to grips with this problem. The main impact of ideas about the political implications of calling, or 'labelling', certain forms of behaviour as deviant came in the 1960s. These ideas were part of a wider interest in the growth of bureaucratic society and its capacity for social control (Becker, 1963; Lemert, 1972, esp. pp. 16–17, 62; Taylor et al., 1973). More recently, labelling theory has attracted the attention of people who are interested in understanding the processes which maintain the international economic order. Horesh (1985), for example, argues that 'the universal acceptance of a specialized vocabulary confers on it the respectability of a scientific language and the appearance of objectivity of description'. But he also points out that the language of development is 'generated in an economically dominant culture', the dominant, then, providing the 'only possible portrayal of relationships between nations'. Apart from some nonsensical uses of language, categories such as the 'third world', which have weak empirical foundations, also carry moral overtones about political and economic arrangements. Similarly to the sociologists of deviance, Wood (1985) also shows how a whole range of particular categorizations used in the language of development and aid involve ideas about domination, subordination, stigmatism and so on, from which it is difficult for the person or group so labelled to escape. These writers are not arguing that it is possible to avoid labelling; labelling is, of necessity, universal and all labelling has political implications. As Wood points out, the question is not 'why label?', but 'which label?' and 'who chooses it?'

The problems discussed here, then, are universal. The next two sections will deal with their specific implications for writing and teaching about women and society. The main points of connection between these problems and their implications are: the use of specific words of denotation, our sense of history and our ideas about disciplinary organization – itself a form of categorization. It is argued here that political science, although it may be the last to do so, could be the most suitable of disciplines for dealing with women's studies.

The sociology of language, women's studies and political studies

Words of denotation

It may seem either 'old hat' or irritating to examine usages of 'he' and 'she'. But it is curious that, while it is academically respectable to discuss the ideological implications of the pronouns of address, it is not so to do this with the third person pronouns. The familiar response to feminists is that any educated person knows that 'he' means 'he and she' except when otherwise stated, that this is a settled and universally accepted grammatical convention. Grammarians often point out that established grammatical rules are frequently the arbitrary decisions of their nineteenth-century predecessors.[5] The nineteenth century reveals a degree of uncertainty about the norm for using both the third person pronouns and related nouns and adjectives. When J.S. Mill failed to get the 1867 Reform Act to refer explicitly to persons (so as to include women voters) a supporter consoled him by pointing to an earlier statute, which stated that all laws referring to 'males' should be read as applying to women. Yet Disraeli made it clear that he believed that the judges would take the view that 'he', 'men' and 'males' did *not* include 'she', 'women' and 'females' (Sachs and Hoff Wilson, 1978: 23). If it were true that there is agreement in the twentieth century about the meanings of pronouns, women would have applied for jobs, places at colleges and so on, even where advertisements said 'he'. This did not happen. Moreover, if it were true that the use of pronouns was uncontentious, it would be unlikely that writers would feel it necessary to make a deliberate choice of an alternative convention, risking adverse comments from reviewers. But when a child psychologist referred in her work on children to 'she' and 'her', the majority of the subjects being female, her 'provocative' pronoun usage was noted as often as her substantive findings.[6] Brown and Gilman (1960) argue that challenges to established use are often ridiculed because they are also challenges to established power. They also point out that the twin controversies of pronoun use and power relations have been resolved in England by the use of the plural 'you'. Often, the plural construction 'they', could be used in place of the singular third person pronouns.

Ambiguities revealed in disputes about the meaning of nouns in the 1867 Reform Act continue into the twentieth century. These exist whether or not the nouns have formal gender connotations and affect our understanding of the social world (a systematic account is provided by Spender, 1980). There is a riddle which used to be popular about a father driving with his son. Following an accident, both are taken to hospital where the surgeon brought in for the child exclaims: 'I can't operate on that child. He is my son.' People used not to be able to explain the riddle because of an unconscious assumption that surgeons were men. Although the riddle may not produce the same effect today, there are still courses taught about human nature with titles such as *Man and Society* which, undoubtedly unintentionally, can perpetuate such imagery. In such courses, treatment of women is likely to be confined to a few specific sessions. Although the general purpose may be to explore basic ideas about human nature which give rise to theories about economic and social rationality, altruism, gender relations and so on, the effect may be to reduce the significance of women as members of the human community. Not only course title and structures but also unreflective use of clichés such as 'economic man' and 'rational man' imply to students, in my experience, that allegedly universal, and therefore important, human characteristics are actually male not female. Even liberal male members of staff may find objections to these features of such courses faintly ridiculous; but I have found that some, not all, male students fail to attend during the weeks on women because they believe these sessions to be less important than the others.

The question of history
The 'special' treatment described above reflects a common belief that men make history. If the sociologists of language are correct about written language and the past, this belief exists because history is recorded as though men make history. This affects not just our 'factual' knowledge but also our sense of what is 'natural'. According to J.S. Mill, what is 'natural' is what is 'customary' (see also Millett on Ruskin, both quoted in Radcliffe Richards, 1980: 45). What we believe has been customary must depend on what we are told. Our written accounts of history tell us not only that women were not political thinkers, or contributors to cultural life, but also that this was 'natural'.

In fact, however, the poverty of our inheritance lies not so much in either the 'natural' or 'factual' absence of 'great women in history' but is the result of other factors. In some ways the reason for the poverty seems analogous to Bernstein's (1970) explanation for the loss of creative working class knowledge; that is, middle class control of linguistic rules and conventions. For example, Spender (1983) shows how the thoughts, artistic talents and political action of women since the fourteenth century have been downgraded or forgotten as the result of reviews and biographies alleging plagiarism, personalization and perverted sexuality (see also commentary in de Pizan, 1983; and Women's Studies International Forum, 1983). Sometimes the reason for the poverty seems to be another, if slightly different, case of Bernstein's claim that the production and dissemination of knowledge is controlled by a dominant class. For example, it has been argued that publishers and editors (often male) omit significant arguments in special re-issues of older works, making them less coherent and, therefore, less persuasive (WSIF, 1983, in which it is also shown that women have been excluded from the trades and crafts used in book production). Although these things appear to have happened most systematically in what is called 'literature', it is important to note that it is often in 'literary' works that women have theorized about female political and social roles (e.g. from de Pizan to Wollstonecraft to de Beauvoir). The 'disappearance' of older works from established bodies of literature means that, as Stimpson points out, women have to 're-invent the wheel' every fifty years (Spender, 1983: 13).

Disciplinary organization
It is perhaps not surprising that some analysts of development issues should be the first social scientists to deal systematically with the political implications of systems of categorization. There are perhaps two reasons for this. Firstly, it is an interdisciplinary subject; or, at least, the impetus has come from those who see their subject as an interdisciplinary one (this may not include 'straight' development economists but does involve 'women's' subjects such as sociology and social anthropology). Consequently, there is probably less fixed agreement about categorizations. Secondly, the processes denoted by the criticized categories developed in dominant cultures, together with the work of the naming institutions such as the World Bank and the situations of the 'labelled', comprise the very subject of the discipline itself. Women's studies is like development studies in the sense that it also draws on several disciplines such as economics, sociology and politics (as well as literature, psychology and philosophy). But there is a difference. Although the impetus for scepticism comes from the radical strand of development studies, it does come from the inside; from established practitioners of the discipline who want to do a better job. Criticisms of research frameworks and language about women, however, come less from those in a position to choose the 'labels', but still largely from the

'outside' or the edges of the academic hierarchy (see Lovenduski, 1981, on women and political science). Political science, could, however, be like development studies; the possibilities for responding to feminist challenges and, in so doing, to improve the discipline, are already there.

The difficulty to be fully overcome lies not just in the general observation (of which women are particularly aware) that 'Aristotelian categorisations of knowledge do not correspond very directly with common experiences' (Goody and Watt, 1963: 343)[7] but is also the specific fact that Aristotle's distinction between the public and the private has been a powerful influence in thinking about what constitutes politics and, hence, political science. This has been compounded by a more recent disciplinary division of labour; separating political science from political economy and political philosophy. The first has led to an emphasis on state institutions as the proper units of analysis in political science, defining the private as personal and non-political. The second has discouraged attention by political scientists (instead of economists and philosophers) from those areas in which the private might have been construed as political. For example, the informal processes of markets, family relationships and conceptions of human nature also give rise to particular distributions of power in the public sphere. Unfortunately, no discipline seems to have escaped Aristotelian assumptions about women and the non-political nature of the private sphere they supposedly inhabit. Even when politics has been re-defined informally as 'who gets what, when and how', the influences on 'what women get, when and how' have been assumed to be outside the boundaries of political science.

But as Randall (1983: 39) points out, Laswell's definition is eminently suitable for taking account of the feminist view that the personal is political; that household and sexual politics are part of the distributive process. Furthermore, policies affecting the household, children and family relationships are as political as those about defence, transport and foreign policy.

There are other 'mainstream' disciplinary developments which beg political science to deal systematically with women. For example, the type of policy analysis recommended by Ashford (ed., 1978: 12–14, 82–3) is justified because it illuminates 'power relationships across societies'; theories of agenda-setting, the 'mobilisation of bias' non-decision-making and the notion of the 'third face' of power, arising out of interest in other forms of inequality, are highly relevant to the treatment of women both in politics and in political science.[8] If political science is about values, socialization, ideologies, power, interests and informal (as well as formal) institutions, to do its job properly it can and ought to be a significant source of research on and teaching about women. If it is to be so, we need to think about literature and course organization.

The future for women's studies and political studies

Literature
At least three strands of change are already obvious: (1) filling the historical 'blanks'; (2) filling gaps in current literature; and (3) assuming as legitimate so-called 'women's' issues as case study material in works on pressure groups, policies, institutions, and so on.

As far as the first is concerned, the actual task is not obviously one for the political scientist. For our own writing and for teaching we ought to look out for works such as Spender's (1983) and to resist dismissing them, before reading, as feminist propaganda. We should also use re-interpretations of already popular areas of research. For example, Banks's (1981) careful and stimulating account of nineteenth-century feminism gives a historical coherence to the modern women's movement that cannot easily be gained from many other works which concentrate on the personalities of leading figures in the suffrage campaigns. The review articles by Randall (1983) and Vallance (1982) discuss several examples of works under the second and third headings. Vallance identifies four main areas where considerable work has been done: women's participation at work, women's participation in public life, the policies of abortion and reproduction and, finally, political theory. Research by both Randall (1982) and Vallance (1979) themselves fill gaps and show how 'women's issues' are as 'mainstream' as other works on pressure groups, institutions and policies. There is increasingly no justification for arguments once heard that there is no academic, only polemical, literature on women.

In writing about women and politics, there are at least two considerations that must be borne in mind. Firstly, the question of authorship is sometimes delicate. Just as members of the Black power movement felt that white people, because of their different experience, could not write about racial discrimination, so some feminists think that men cannot write about women. From a methodological point of view, the controversy parallels that between the positivists and the Verstehen and participant observer schools.[9] For academic women there is an added political twist: the possibility of being accused of exploiting understandings reached in women's groups to succeed by men's standards in a men's world. At the same time, in that man's world they and some men may well be put down for going in for a 'soft-option' (Vallance, 1982: 582). Decisions by writers and potential writers, about what to do and how to do it, necessarily involve social as well as intellectual considerations, at least for the time being.

From the more unambiguously academic point of view, it is important to avoid the 'Women and . . .' syndrome. The pitfalls are described by a man, Tomlinson (see also Bezucha, 1985: 91 on Lerner's 'add women and stir'), as:

> . . .a common scenario on the left in Britain. A man gives a paper to a socialist conference about socialist economic policy. He is politely but trenchantly criticised by a woman for not dealing with (indeed barely mentioning) women. The temptation then open is for that man to go away and 'add in' women producing the common format of the paper 'Women and X' where X is a traditional socialist policy and women are an after-thought. (Tomlinson 1984: 45)

Women as an afterthought is not much of an advance on older works in which women are a footnote or perhaps even a paragraph. None of these approaches, unlike the works reviewed or written by Randall and Vallance, integrate the study of women with main bodies of knowledge on, for example, work, participation and policy in a way that both enriches the general texts and increases the literature on women. Analogous issues about 'special' treatment and 'women as afterthoughts' also occur in course organization.

Course organization
There are three ways of teaching about the politics of women:

(1)   separate women's studies courses to which there is a politics input;
(2)   specific weeks devoted to women in general politics courses;
(3)   integration into all courses of ideas that 'women's issues are as relevant as 'men's' and no less political in questions of citizen-ship, electoral systems, participation, representation and substantive policy areas, and so on.

Examples of the first are given in a recent European Community publication (Commission of the European Communities, 1985), which identifies about twenty British places of higher education which have undergraduate courses on women or gender relations. About fourteen colleges or universities offer postgraduate women's studies diploma or degree programmes. This approach has succeeded in ensuring that previously excluded topics are on the agenda, particularly in view of the recent expansion of such courses. As a result of their commitment to a so-called soft option, those who teach such courses and students may be isolated or denied esteem. Several writers in a collection of essays edited by Culley and Portuges (1985) are especially concerned about the marginalization of Black women's studies. The existence of a women's studies course may lead also to a complacent view that there is no need to alter other courses. Furthermore, if there is no strong administrative home for separate courses, such as a faculty, it is possible that contributing staff may feel obliged to treat them with lower priority than their own discipline's courses. Finally, institutions which do not have women's studies courses already are likely to resist their introduction. Pressure on resources is producing strict rules about course proliferation at the undergraduate level and increasing competition for fewer student awards limits the prospect for new postgraduate taught programmes. At the research level, all projects, however scholarly, which do not bring in large external funds to universities and colleges are being squeezed out.

In view of the problems affecting taught courses, many academics try to allocate elsewhere specific weeks and a couple of essay questions to women's rights and their role in society. That is good in that it does indicate that people are aware that there is a gap but marginalization of the politics of women may occur here as much as in special courses; perhaps more so by reducing women to, say, two weeks instead of ten or more. That this tells students that women are correspondingly less important than men is indicated by my experience of reasons for non-attendance during courses such as *Man and Society*.

To go for the third possibility would cost least in resources and is least likely to arouse controversy in the wider institutional set-up. And it seems, in some ways, the best; in the long run it is the most likely way of conveying the view that women are as normal as men in their membership of the political community. It would cost least because it need not involve new appointments, extra teaching, and so on. It would be uncontroversial in the sense that most academics have some freedom to teach what they like within the frameworks of the rubrics, syllabuses, and so on that go to boards of studies and senates. And it is intellectually coherent, given what has been said earlier about developments in what counts as politics and political science.

There are, however, counter-arguments which lend support for a combination of separation, despite its possible drawbacks, and reform from within. If administratively easy and professionally sensible, the latter approach is likely to be ideologically difficult. It is hard for people to escape habitual ways of thinking about their discipline and about what are to be regarded as basic texts on their bibliographies. But it is quite possible that bibliographies given to students need revision. This may be resisted as it was at one university in the late 1970s, where female students themselves had to go through catalogues and modernize bibliographies for courses in politics, philosophy and economics. Indeed, some writers argue that integration of this type is impossible; that it is a misnomer for assimilation. Raymond (1985), for example, argues that the general disciplinary division we know today is the result of the pursuit of autonomy by subjects such as political science from its relatives, economics and philosophy. Likewise positive separation – rather than separation imposed by others – of women's studies from other disciplines is the only way for it, too, to achieve integration in the alternative sense of having its own 'original unity' of methods, traditions, values and content. Disagreements about separation, integration or assimilation also appear in ideas about women's participation in public life. These are connected to competing theories, discussed below, about the source of inequality between women and men and, as a result, what steps are needed to alter the distribution of power.

Women's studies, political studies and political practice

It was argued in the beginning that there is a connection for everyone between language and our understanding of social experience; a dialectical one, at any rate, if not a uni-causal one. As far as academics are concerned, there is growing agreement that the systematic pursuit and communication of knowledge is not a neutral process, even in the natural sciences where there may be the greatest justification for a claim that the facts analysed are objective. The argument is that, even if the positivists are right (and this is disputed) about the neutrality of enquiry, the requirement to make findings available for scrutiny by others has political implications. The reason is not simply that there are distortions arising from the need to make careers and secure funds (Wade and Broad, 1982) but that the findings no longer 'belong' to the researcher. They have been placed in the public domain for others to use and to do this is to commit a social or political act.[10]

It would be arrogant to suggest that the way in which we theorize, systematize and communicate knowledge about women fully determines the political experience of women. We are all familiar with the ready reference of politicians to traditional ways of thinking about women to justify different treatment under nationality laws and in strategies for dealing with unemployment. But it has been pointed out often that the fact that traditional modes do not fully correspond with women's experience[11] encourages their rejection and receptivity by women to alternative ways of thinking. Nevertheless, there is evidence that the disjunction between experience and conventional ideas in the 1960s first produced only inchoate resentments (Randall, 1982). Dominant ideas about women and family life, communicated through books and other media, made dissatisfaction seem a personal rather than a public problem (Friedan, 1963). It was the discovery of writings by feminist theorists ('re-inventing the wheel' in the 1960s) that enabled the dissatisfied to see the explanation in institutional or structural terms.

However, there are mutually incompatible theories about the 'privatization' of women. Broadly speaking, these fall into two types.[12] On the one hand, there is the idea that the Aristotelian separation of the private and public spheres and the confinement of women to the former[13] is not 'natural'. The dispositions and characteristics of women that are used to justify this arrangement are, to use J.S. Mill's words, 'forced artificially or unnaturally' by social institutions (quoted in Radcliffe Richards, 1980: 45). Reform the institutions and it is possible to have a society in which the private and the public are merged and women and men are equally free to participate as they choose in all aspects of life. There are both liberal and socialist versions of this theory. On the other hand, there is the view that women and men are, indeed, distinctly and unalterably different. Furthermore, this theory rests on the view (also held by some anti-feminists) that women are naturally morally superior to men. Domination of the superior by the inferior, in liberal and socialist societies, is explained by reference to the theory of patriarchy. Its implications are separatism and even sexual apartheid, for academic and political practice.

At one level, the separatist theory has its attractions. Examples abound of successful 'token' women abandoning 'women's' issues and distancing themselves from other women because success in a 'men's world' necessitates behaving like a man. And, in addition to Raymond's argument cited earlier, there are good psychological reasons for women-only groups in schools and colleges, as in politics, to escape the internalization of assumptions that men are cleverer, better at talking, and so on, and to provide bases for the development of similar confidence and skills in women. But, as Evans points out, there is little evidence that women are innately morally superior (1984) and, hence, little support or justification for an opposite pattern of domination. Apart from moral objections to such an alternative society, there are practical reasons for rejecting even simple separation as a complete or long-term solution. Existing structures of male power will not disappear if women ignore them and, since they dominate, they will continue to affect women's lives through their policies and the systems of knowledge on which these are based. Past experience of separate treatment has not shown itself to be a system of equal treatment (*Plessy v Ferguson* to *Brown v Board of Education*). And, on the contrary, even if change is painfully slow, there is some indication that institutions can be influenced by feminist ideas developed in women's groups. Vallance (1979) discusses this in connection with Parliament. Trade unions finally added practical rather than rhetorical weight to campaigns for equal pay only after it became clear that women were becoming unionized and militant (Randall, 1982; Meehan, 1985). These political examples seem to reinforce the earlier academic arguments for both reform within the discipline of political science and some separation from it.

The people we teach are the people who, tomorrow, will be participants in all those institutions which limit women's autonomy. We teach men as well as women. Therefore, we need to ensure that the courses men take, as well as those that women take, question their assumptions about women as much as their assumptions about anything else. Higher education at its best is supposed, after all, to question everything. Thus, for the sake of both political science and women, we need to ensure that our discipline deals fully with all members of society and with all political processes and relationships. The immediate task is at least three-fold. It is necessary to recognize: that there are politics in the private sphere; that those who are assumed to inhabit the private sphere are also participants in the public; and that public policies directed at the private sphere are no less political or important than those aimed at the public. Ultimately, the social force of the analytical distinction as it is now between the two spheres will become as redundant as the attempt to determine how many angels can dance on the head of a pin. This need not entail the loss of a sense of difference between civil society and the state. Arguing against both conservative and Marxist denials of such difference, Rodger (1985) proposes a reconstitution of the public sphere that acknowledges a necessary contribution to the expansion of political debate by social movements which may have no formal roles in public institutions. He cites the ecology and anti-nuclear campaigns. In view of the specific points made earlier about Parliament and the trade unions and in view of the wider feminist ideas about the personal and the political, a proper reconstruction of the public sphere cannot take place without feminist theory.

Notes

In writing this chapter, it has been rewarding to find that thinking about women's studies and feminist theory has compelled me to synthesize what, in some ways, have seemed to be rather disparate interests in epistemology, the sociology of knowledge, political institutions, policy-making and constitutional questions as well as women's roles in society. I am grateful to past teachers for their stimulation in these various.

areas and to Bob Benewick for his invitation to present a paper from which this chapter has grown, in his panel on Critical Political Science at the Political Studies Annual Conference in 1985, and for the discussion that ensued. I am also grateful to Brian Morton and Brian Smith for their help in the production of a shorter version which appeared in the *Times Higher Education Supplement* on 26 April 1985. What has been invaluable are the comments and help received from members of the Women and Politics Groups of the PSA at the Annual Conference and in preparation of this final version.

1. Readers should refer to the two reviews for titles of books discussed by Vallance and Randall. The subjects covered range over womens' participation at work, and in public life, the politics of abortion and reproduction and political theory.

2. I am also grateful to Professor Roy Edgley, formerly of Sussex University, for his philosophy lectures in 1975–6 on this problem.

3. Another illustration is the way in which 'snow' is named in different languages. Eskimos, whose survival depends on expert knowledge of different types of snow, have many names for its different manifestations. In societies where snow is rarer, names for it are fewer.

4. For example, the Black power movement and its phrase 'Black is beautiful'. At the same time, there were reassessments in the then Commonwealth Office about which categorizations had acquired insulting connotations and what re-naming was necessary.

5. For example, the weekly lexicographer's column, 'Words', in *The Observer* regularly reveals instances.

6. A. Antonelli, Seminar, British Sociological Association, S.W. Women's Caucus, Bristol University, 1980.

7. For a full discussion of this see J.B. Elshtain (1974). Briefly, Aristotle made a distinction between the public and private spheres; the former being the realm of political institutions, the law, rational and disinterested discussion of public affairs and the latter being the realm of private arrangements, emotions and feelings. The state was the highest form of social organization to which others were subordinate. The household was a refuge or haven in the private sphere for those whose duty it was to participate in the public. Aristotle also believed that men and women had innately different characteristics such as rationality and sensitivity, respectively. These, in his view, justified a public sphere inhabited by men only and confinement of women to the private sphere. Men, however, could display 'feminine' behaviour when acting in the private sphere and still be 'good' men. But women if they tried to enter the public sphere, would have to exhibit 'masculine' traits and this would make them 'bad' women. Banks (1981) shows how this view reached an apotheosis in nineteenth-century Britain; elements are still frequently found in public references to working women and female politicians.

8. All of these involve arguments that socialization processes, ideology and the nature of political institutions serve to limit the articulation, or even consciousness, of subordinate class or group interests and, hence, to discourage challenges to the existing distribution of power. See, for example, Schattschneider (1960), Bachrach and Barratz (1962, 1963), and Lukes (1974).

9. This dispute is about what constitutes objective knowledge and which research methods are likely to maximize real understandings of social phenomena. There is a related debate between positivists and behaviourists, on the one hand, and the interpretivist school of philosophy, on the other, about whether proper explanations are causal or semantic. For positivists, the observer is detached and neutral, making value-

free observations of the causes of social events. Participant observers, believing that knowledge is contextual with culture, seek an empathetic understanding of the society under scrutiny. The interpretivists, following Wittgenstein, believe that social phenomena are not fully understood unless the meaning of an action is understood in relation to the general theories governing the society in which the action is taking place. A good explanation of the importance of understanding differences in the meaning of participation is provided by Schwartz (1984). See also Giddens (1976) and Maher (1985).

10. Again, I am grateful to Professor Edgley for his philosophy lecturers at Sussex University in 1975–6.

11. See note 7. The fact that women have found that what was irrational was not themselves but rules, and justifications for them, which barred them from voting and entering certain occupations is an illustration of the general point about lack of correspondence made by Goody and Watt (1963).

12. More extended discussion of them can be found in Elshtain (1974), Banks (1981), Randall (1982), Vallance (1982) and Evans (1984).

13. See note 7.

References

Ashford, D. (ed.) (1978) *Comparing Public Policies*. Beverly Hills: Sage.

Bachrach, P. and M. Barratz (1962) 'Two Faces of Power', *American Political Science Review*, 56(4): 947–52.

Bachrach, P. and M. Barratz (1963) 'Decisions and Non-decisions: an Analytical Framework', *American Political Science Review*, 57(3): 632–42.

Banks, O. (1981) *Faces of Feminism*. Oxford: Martin Robertson.

Beauvoir, S. de (1952 edition) *The Second Sex*, H. Parshley (trans.). New York: Alfred Knopf.

Becker, H. (1963) *Outsiders*. Toronto: Collier-Macmillan.

Bernstein, B. (1970) 'Social Class, Language and Socialisation', pp. 157–78 in P. Giglioli (ed.) (1972), *Language and Social Context*. Harmondsworth: Penguin.

Bezucha, R. (1985) 'Feminist Pedagogy as a Subversive Activity', pp. 81–95 in M. Culley and C. Portuges (eds), *Gendered Subjects: The Dynamics of Feminist Teaching*. Boston, London, Melbourne and Henley: Routledge.

Boals, K. and R. Klein (eds) (1983) *Theories of Women's Studies*. London: Routledge.

Bonder, G. (1983) 'The Study of Politics from the Standpoint of Women', *International Social Science Journal*, XXV(4): 569–83.

Bonder, G. (1985) 'The Educational Process of Women's Studies in Argentina: Reflections on Theory and Technique', pp. 64–77 in M. Culley and C. Portuges (eds), *Gendered Subjects: The Dynamics of Feminist Teaching*. Boston, London, Melbourne and Henley: Routledge.

Brand, G. (ed.) (1979) *The Central Texts of Ludwig Wittgenstein*. Oxford: Blackwell.

Brown, R. and A. Gilman (1960) 'The Pronouns of Power and Solidarity', pp. 252–82 in P. Giglioli (ed.) (1972), *Language and Social Context*. Harmondsworth: Penguin.

Butler, J. (1985) 'Towards a Pedagogy of Everywoman's Studies', pp. 230–39 in M. Culley and C. Portuges (eds), *Gendered Subjects: The Dynamics of Feminist Teaching*. Boston, London, Melbourne and Henley: Routledge.

Cocks, J. (1985) 'Suspicious Pleasures: on Teaching Feminist Theory', pp. 171–82 in M. Culley and C. Portuges (eds), *Gendered Subjects: The Dynamics of Feminist Teaching*. Boston, London, Melbourne and Henley: Routledge.

Commission of the European Communities (1985) 'Women's Studies', *Women of Europe*, Supplement 18.

Culley, M. and C. Portuges (eds), *Gendered Subjects: The Dynamics of Feminist Teaching*. Boston, London, Melbourne and Henley: Routledge.

Elshtain, J.B. (1974) 'Moral Woman and Immoral Man: a Consideration of the Public–Private Split and its Political Ramifications', *Politics and Society*, 4(4): 453–73.

Evans, J. (1980) 'Attitudes towards Women in American Political Science', *Government and Opposition*, 15(1): 101–14.

Evans, J. (1984) 'The Good Society? Implications of a Greater Participation of Women in Public Life', *Political Studies*, XXXII(4): 618–26.

Featherman, S. (1985) 'Designing a Course on Women in American Politics. A Focus on Power and Conflict', *News for Teachers of Political Science* (Publication of the American Political Science Association), 45 (Spring): 10–11.

Friedan, B. (1963) *The Feminist Mystique*. Harmondsworth: Penguin.

Friedan, B. (1977) *It Changed My Life*. New York: Dell.

Friedman, S. (1985) 'Authority in the Feminist Classroom: a Contradiction in Terms?' pp. 202–8 in M. Culley and C. Portuges (eds), *Gendered Subjects: The Dynamics of Feminist Teaching*. Boston, London, Melbourne and Henley: Routledge.

Giddens, A. (1976) *New Rules of Sociological Method*. London: Hutchinson.

Giglioli, P. (ed.) (1972) *Language and Social Context*. Harmondsworth: Penguin.

Goody, J. and I. Watt (1963) 'The Consequences of Literacy', pp. 311–57 in P. Giglioli (ed.) (1972) *Language and Social Context*. Harmondsworth: Penguin.

Horesh, E. (1985) 'Labelling and the Language of International Development', in G. Wood (ed.) *Labelling in Development Policy*. London and Beverly Hills: Sage.

Lemert, E. (1972) *Human Deviance, Social Problems and Social Control*. Boston, London, Melbourne and Henley: Routledge.

Lovenduski, J. (1981) *Women in British Political Studies*. Glasgow, Centre for Study of Political Studies: Political Studies Association.

Lukes, S. (1974) *Power: A Radical View*. London: Macmillan.

Maher, F. (1985) 'Classroom Pedagogy and the New Scholarship on Women', pp. 29–38 in M. Culley and C. Portuges (eds), *Gendered Subjects: The Dynamics of Feminist Teaching*. Boston, London, Melbourne and Henley: Routledge.

Meehan, E. (1985) *Women's Rights at Work: Campaigns and Policy in Britain and the United States*. London: Macmillan.

Pizan, C. de (1983 edition) *The Book of the City of Ladies*, E. Richards (trans.) with commentary by M. Warner. London: Picador.

Radcliffe Richards, J. (1980) *The Sceptical Feminist*. London, Boston, Melbourne and Henley: Routledge.

Randall, V. (1982) *Women and Politics*. London: Macmillan.

Randall, V. (1983) 'Teaching about Women and Politics', *Politics*, 3(1): 38–43.

Raymond, J. (1985) 'Women's Studies: a Knowledge of One's Own', pp. 49–63 in M. Culley and C. Portuges (eds), *Gendered Subjects: The Dynamics of Feminist Teaching*. Boston, London, Melbourne and Henley: Routledge.

Rich, A. (1985) 'Taking Women Students Seriously', pp. 21–8 in M. Culley and C. Portuges (eds), *Gendered Subjects: The Dynamics of Feminist Teaching*. Boston, London, Melbourne and Henley: Routledge.

Rifkin, J. (1985) 'Teaching Mediation: a Feminist Perspective on the Study of Law', pp. 96–100 in M. Culley and C. Portuges (eds), *Gendered Subjects; the Dynamics of Feminist Teaching*. Boston, London, Melbourne and Henley: Routledge.

Rodger, J. (1985) 'On the Degeneration of the Public Sphere', *Political Studies*, XXXII(2): 203–17.

Sachs, A. and J. Hoff Wilson (1978) *Sexism and the Law*. London: Martin Robertson.

Schattschneider, E. (1960) *The Semi-Sovereign People*. New York: Rinehart & Winston.

Schwartz, J. (1984) 'Participation and Multisubjective Understanding: an Interpretivist Approach to the Study of Political Participation', *The Journal of Politics*, 46(4): 1117–41.

Spelman, E. (1985) 'Combatting the Marginalisation of Black Women in the Classroom', pp. 240–44 in M. Culley and C. Portuges (eds), *Gendered Subjects: The Dynamics of Feminist Teaching*. Boston, London, Melbourne and Henley: Routledge.

Spender, D. (1980) *Man Made Language*. London: Routledge.

Spender, D. (1983) *Women of Ideas and What Men Have Done to Them*. London: Routledge.

Taylor, P., P. Walton and J. Young (1973) *The New Criminology*. London and Boston: Routledge.

Tomlinson, J. (1984) 'Incomes Policies and Women's Wages', *M/F*, 9: 45–58.

Vallance, E. (1979) *Women in the House*. London: Athlone.

Vallance, E. (1982) 'Writing Women Back In', *Political Studies*, XXX(4): 582–90.

Wade, N. and W. Broad (1982) *Betrayers of the Truth*. New York: Simon & Schuster.

Wittgenstein, L. (1979) *The Central Texts of Ludwig Wittgenstein*. G. Brand (ed.). Oxford: Blackwell.

Wollstonecraft, M. (1983 edition) *Vindication of the Rights of Women*. Harmondsworth: Penguin.

Women's Studies International Forum (WSIF) (1983) *Gatekeeping: The Denial, Dismissal and Distortion of Women*. Special Issue 6(5).

Wood, G. (1985) 'The Politics of Development Policy Labelling' in G. Wood (ed.), *Labelling in Development Policy*. London and Beverly Hills: Sage.

Wood, G. (1985) 'Target Strikes Back' in G. Wood (ed.), *Labelling in Development Policy*. London and Beverly Hills: Sage.

Bibliography

Abrams, M.H. (1971) *Natural Supernaturalism. Tradition and Revolution in Romantic Literature*. New York: W.W. Norton.

Ariès, P. (1962) *Centuries of Childhood*. London: Jonathan Cape.

Ardener, S. (ed.) (1981) *Perceiving Woman*. London: Dent.

Ashford, D. (ed.) (1978) *Comparing Public Policies*. Beverly Hills: Sage.

Assiter, A. (1985) 'Did Man Make Language', pp. 310–21 in R. Edgeley and R. Osborne (eds), *Radical Philosophy Reader*. London: Verso.

Bachrach, P. and M. Barratz (1962) 'Two Faces of Power', *American Political Science Review*, 56(4): 947–52.

Bachrach, P. and M. Barratz (1963) 'Decisions and Non-Decisions: an Analytical Perspective', *American Political Science Review*, 57: 632–42.

Banks, O. (1981) *Faces of Feminism*. Oxford: Martin Robertson.

Barnes, J. (n.d.) *The Case for Women's Rights*. Society for Libertarian Life.

Barrett, M. (1980) *Women's Oppression Today: Problems in Marxist Feminist Analysis*. London: Verso.

Barrett, M. and M. MacIntosh (1982) *The Anti-Social Family*. London: Verso.

Bax, E.B. (1913) *The Fraud of Feminism*. London: Grant Richards.

Beauvoir, S. de (1952 edition) *The Second Sex*, H. Parshley (trans.). New York: Alfred Knopf.

Bebel, A. (1971) *Woman under Socialism*. New York: Schocken Books (reprint of translation by Daniel De Leon, 1904).

Becker, H. (1963) *Outsiders*. Toronto: Collier-Macmillan.

Beecham, D. (1980) 'The Ruling Class Offensive', *International Socialism*, 6(4): 1–18.

Beecham, D. (1983) 'Get the Tories Out', *Socialist Review*, 54(2): 3–6.

Beechey, V. (1979) 'On Patriarchy', *Feminist Review*, 3.

Benn, S. and S. Gaus (eds) (1983) *Public and Private in Social Life*. London: Croom Helm.

Bernstein, B. (1970) 'Social Class, Language and Socialisation', pp. 157–78 in P. Giglioli (ed.), *Language and Social Context*. Harmondsworth: Penguin.

Bleaney, M. (1983) 'Conservative Economic Strategy', pp. 132–47 in S. Hall and M. Jacques (eds), *The Politics of Thatcherism*. London: Lawrence & Wishart.

Bloch, M. and J.H. Bloch (1980) 'Women and the Dialectics of Nature in Eighteenth Century French Thought', pp. 25–41 in C. McCormack and M. Strathern (eds), *Nature, Culture and Gender*. Cambridge: Cambridge University Press.

Boals, K. (1975) 'Review: Political Science', *Signs*, I(1): 161–74.

Bonder, G. (1983) 'The Study of Politics from the Standpoint of Women', *International Social Science Journal*, XXV(4): 569–83.

Bouchier, D. (1983) *The Feminist Challenge*. London: Macmillan.

Bowles, G. and R. Klein (eds) (1983) *Theories of Women's Studies*. London: Routledge.

Boxer, M. and J. Quataert (eds) (1978) *Socialist Women: European Socialist Feminism in the Nineteenth and Early Twentieth Centuries*. New York: Elsevier.

Brand, G. (ed.) (1979) *The Central Texts of Ludwig Wittgenstein*. Oxford: Blackwell.

Breines, P. (1968) 'Marxism and the New Left in America', in J. Habermas (ed.), *Antworfen auf Herbert Marcuse*. Frankfurt: Surhrkump Verlag.

Brennan, T. and C. Pateman (1979) 'Mere auxiliaries to the Commonwealth', *Political Studies*, XXVII(2): 183–200.

Brittan, S. (1980) 'Hayek, the New Right and the Crisis of Social Democracy', *Encounter*, 54(1): 31–46.

Bromley, P. (1977) *Family Law*. London: Butterworth.

Brown, R. and A. Gilman (1960) 'The Pronouns of Power and Solidarity', pp. 252–82 in P. Giglioli (ed.) (1972) *Language and Social Context*. Harmondsworth: Penguin.

Brownmiller, S. (1976) *Against our Will*. Harmondsworth: Penguin.

Buhle, M.J. (1981) *Women and American Socialism 1870–1920*. Springfield, IL: University of Illinois Press.

Bull, D. and P. Wilding (eds) (1983) *Thatcherism and the Poor*. London: Child Poverty Action Group.

Cameron, D. and L. Fraser (1984) 'The Liberal Organ: Needs, Rights and Pornography in the *Guardian*', *Trouble and Strife*, 4: 23–7.

CHANGE (1981) *Military Ideology and the Dissolution of Democracy. Women in Chile*. London: CHANGE International Reports.

Chesler, P. (1972) *Women and Madness*. London: Allen Lane.

Cixous, H. (1981) extract from 'Sorties', pp. 90–8 in E. Marks and I. de Courtrivon (eds), *New French Feminism*. Brighton: Harvester.

Clark, L.M.G. and L. Lange (1979) *The Sexism of Social and Political Theory: Women and Reproduction from Plato to Nietzsche*. Toronto: University of Toronto Press.

Collins, H. (1971) 'The Marxism of the Social Democratic Federation', pp. 46–69 in A. Briggs and J. Saville (eds) *Essays in Labour History 1886–1923*. London: Macmillan.

Commission of the European Communities (1985) 'Women's Studies', *Women of Europe*. Supplement 18.

Condorcet (1976) 'On the Admission of Women to the Rights of Citizenship,' pp. 97–104 in Condorcet, *Selected Writings* K.M. Baker (ed.). Indianapolis: Bobbs-Merrill (first published 1790).

Coote, A. and B. Campbell (1982) *Sweet Freedom*. Oxford: Blackwell.

Coward, R. (1983) *Patriarchal Precedents: Sexuality and Social Relations*. London: Routledge.

Coward, R. and J. Ellis (1977) *Language and Materialism*. London: Routledge.

Crawford, A. (1980) *Thunder on the Right: 'The New Right' and the Politics of Resentment*. New York: Pantheon.

Culley, M. and C. Portuges (eds) (1985) *Gendered Subjects: The Dynamics of Feminist Teaching*. Boston, London, Melbourne and Henley: Routledge.

Daly, M. (1978) *Gyn/Ecology*. London: The Women's Press.

David, M. (1983) 'The New Right in the USA and Britain: A New Anti-feminist Moral Economy', *Critical Social Policy*, 2(3): 21–45.

Davis, M. (1981) 'The New Right's Road to Power', *New Left Review*, 128: 28–49.

Delmar, R. (1979) 'Introduction', in S. Firestone, *The Dialectic of Sex*. London: The Women's Press.

Delphy, C. (1984) *Close to Home: A Materialist Analysis of Women's Oppression*. London: Hutchinson.

Dowse, R. and J. Hughes (eds) (1972) *Political Sociology*. London: Wiley.

Dreitzel, H. (ed.) (1972) *Family, Marriage and the Struggle of the Sexes*. London: Macmillan.

Duncan, G. (ed.) (1983) *Democratic Theory and Practice*. Cambridge: Cambridge University Press.

Dworkin, A. (1983) *Right Wing Women*. London: The Women's Press.

Edholm, F., O. Harris and K. Young (1977) 'Conceptualising Women', *Critique of Anthropology*, 9/10: 101–30.

Ehrenreich, B. (1983) *The Hearts of Men*. London: Pluto.

Eisenstein, H. (1984) *Contemporary Feminist Thought*. London: Hutchinson.

Eisenstein, Z. (1981a) 'Antifeminism in the Politics and Election of 1980', *Feminist Studies*, 7(2): 187–205.

Eisenstein, Z. (1981b) *The Radical Future of Liberal Feminism*. New York: Longman.

Eisenstein, Z. (1982) 'The Sexual Politics of the New Right: Understanding the "Crisis of Liberalism" for the 1980's', *Signs: Journal of Women In Culture and Society*, 7(3): 567–88.

Eisenstein, Z. (ed.) (1979) *Capitalist Patriarchy and the Case for Socialist Feminism*. New York and London: Monthly Review Press.

Elshtain, J. (1974) 'Moral Woman and Immoral Man: a Consideration of the Public/Private Split and its Political Ramifications', *Politics and Society*, 4(4): 453–73.

Elshtain, J. (1981) *Public Man, Private Woman*. Oxford: Martin Robertson.

Elshtain, J. (ed.) (1982) *The Family in Political Thought*. Brighton: Harvester.

Engels, F. (1976 edition) *The Origins of the Family, Private Property and the State*. London: Lawrence & Wishart.

Evans, J. (1980) 'Attitudes to Women in American Political Science', *Government and Opposition*, 15(1): 101–41.

Evans, J. (1984) 'The Good Society? Implications of a Greater Participation by Women in Public Life', *Political Studies*, XXXII(4), 618–26.

Evans, R. (1977) *The Feminists: Women's Emancipation Movements in Europe, America and Australasia 1840–1920*. London: Croom Helm.

Featherman, S. (1985) 'Designing a Course on Women in American Politics. A Focus on Power and Conflict', *News for Teachers of Political Science* (publication of the American Political Science Association), 45(Spring): 10–11.

Firestone, S. (1971) *The Dialectic of Sex*. London: Jonathan Cape (first published 1970).

Fox-Genovese, E. (1977) 'Property and Patriarchy in Classical Bourgeois Political Theory', *Radical History Review*, 4(2–3).

Foxley, A. (1982) 'Towards a Free Market Economy: Chile 1974–1979', *Journal of Development Economics*, 10(1): 1–29.

Friedan, B. (1963) *The Feminist Mystique*. Harmondsworth: Penguin.

Friedan, B. (1977) *It Changed My Life*. New York: Dell.

Friedman, M. (1953) *Essays in Positive Economics*. Chicago: University of Chicago Press.

Friedman, M. (1962) *Capitalism and Freedom*. Chicago: University of Chicago Press.

Friedman, M. (1976) 'The Line We Dare Not Cross: the Fragility of Freedom', *Encounter*, 47(11): 8–15.

Gamble, A. (1979) 'The Free Economy and the Strong State: the Rise of the Social Market Economy', *Socialist Register*, 1–25.

Gamble, A. (1983) 'Thatcherism and Conservative Politics', pp. 109–31 in S. Hall and M. Jacques (eds), *The Politics of Thatcherism*. London: Lawrence & Wishart.

Giddens, A. (1976) *New Rules of Sociological Method*. London: Hutchinson.

Giglioli, P. (ed.) (1972) *Language and Social Context*. Harmondsworth: Penguin.

Glass, J. (1982) 'Kafka and Laing on the Trapped Consciousness', pp. 269–87 in J. Elshtain (ed.), *The Family in Political Thought*. Brighton: Harvester.

Glynn, A. and J. Harrison (1980) *The British Economic Disaster*. London: Pluto.

Gough, I. (1983) 'Thatcherism and the Welfare State', pp. 148–68 in S. Hall and M. Jacques (eds), *The Politics of Thatcherism*. London: Lawrence & Wishart.

Graham, R. (1977) 'Loaves and Liberty: Women in the French Revolution' pp. 263–54 in R. Bridenthal and C. Koonz (eds), *Becoming Visible. Women In European History*. Boston: Houghton Mifflin.

Green, J.P. (1976) *All Men are Created Equal*. Oxford.

Greenleaf, W.H. (1983) *The British Political Tradition*. Vol. 1 *The Ideological Heritage*. London: Methuen.

Greer, G. (1971) *The Female Eunuch*. London: Paladin.

Hall, S. (1982) 'Redrawing the Political Map', *Marxism Today*, December: 14–20.

Hall, S., C. Critcher, T. Jefferson, J. Clarke, B. Roberts (1978) *Policing the Crisis – Mugging, the State and Law and Order*. London: Macmillan.

Hall, S. and M. Jacques (eds) (1983) *The Politics of Thatcherism*. London: Lawrence & Wishart.

Hamilton, R. (1978) *The Liberation of Women: A Study of Patriarchy and Capitalism*. London: Allen & Unwin.

Harrison, B. (1978) *Separate Spheres. The Opposition to Women's Suffrage in Britain*. London: Croom Helm.

Hartmann, H. (1981) 'The Unhappy Marriage of Marxism and Feminism', pp. 1–41 in L. Sargent (ed.), *Women and Revolution: A Discussion of the Unhappy Marriage of Marxism and Feminism*. London: Pluto.

Hartsock, N. (1983) *Money, Sex and Power*. London: Longman.

Haworth, N. and J. Roddick (n.d.) 'Chile 1924 and 1979: Labour Policy and Industrial Relations through Two Revolutions'. Unpublished mimeo.

University of Glasgow.
Hayek, F.A. von (1945) *Individualism True and Fair*. Dublin: 12th Finlay Lecture, University College.
Hayek, F.A. von (1960) *The Constitution of Liberty*. London: Routledge.
Hayek, F.A. von (1967a) 'The Economy, Science and Politics', pp. 251–69 in F.A. Hayek, *Studies in Philosophy, Politics and Economics*. London: Routledge.
Hayek, F.A. von (1967b) 'Principles of a Liberal Social Order', pp. 160–77 in F.A. Hayek, *Studies in Philosophy, Politics and Economics*. London: Routledge.
Hayek, F.A. von (1967c) 'Theory of Complex Phenomena', pp. 22–42 in F.A. Hayek, *Studies in Philosophy, Politics and Economics*. London: Routledge.
Hayek, F.A. von (1973) *Economic Freedom and Representative Government*. London: IEA Occasional Paper. Number 39.
Hayek, F.A. von (1979) *Law, Legislation and Liberty*. Volume 1: *Rules and Order*. London: Routledge.
Hesse, M. (1978) 'Theory and Value in the Social Sciences', pp. 1–16 in C. Hookaway and P. Pettit (eds), *Action and Interpretation*. Cambridge: Cambridge University Press.
Hodgson, G. (1981) *Labour at the Crossroads*. Oxford: Martin Robertson.
Horesh, E. (1985) 'Labelling and the Language of International Development', in G. Wood (ed.), *Labelling in Development Policy.* London and Beverly Hills: Sage.
Hunt, K. (1980) 'Women and the Social Democratic Federation: Some Notes on Lancashire', *North West Labour History Society Bulletin*, 7: 49–64.
Iglitzin, L. (1972a) 'Political Education and Sexual Liberation', *Politics and Society*, II(2): 241–59.
Iglitzin, L. (1972b) 'Sex-typing and Politicization in Children's Attitudes'. Paper presented to the Annual General Meeting of the American Political Science Association.
Jacoby, R. (1977) *Social Amnesia*. Brighton: Harvester.
Jaggar, A. (1983) *Feminist Politics and Human Nature*. Brighton: Harvester.
Jansenn-Jurreit, M. (1982) *Sexism*. London: Pluto.
Jessop. B., K. Bonnett, S. Bromley, T. Ling (1984) 'Authoritarian Populism, Two Nations, and Thatcherism', *New Left Review* 147: 32–61.
Jordan, B. (1982) *Mass Unemployment and the Future of Britain*. Oxford: Blackwell.
Kerber, L. (1980) *Women of the Republic: Intellect and Ideology in Revolutionary America*. Raleigh, NC: University of North Carolina Press.
Kleinbaum, A.R. (1977) 'Women in the Age of Light', pp. 217–35 in R. Bridenthal and C. Koonz (eds), *Becoming Visible. Women in European History*. Boston: Houghton Mifflin.
Krouse, R.W. (1982) 'Patriarchal Liberalism and Beyond: From John Stuart Mill to Harriet Taylor', pp. 145–72 in J. Elshtain (ed.) *The Family in Political Thought*. Brighton: Harvester.
Kuhn, A. and A.M. Wolpe (1978) *Feminism and Materialism*. London: Routledge.

Kuhn, T. (1973) *The Structure of Scientific Revolutions*. Chicago and London: University of Chicago Press.

Leftwich, A. (ed.) (1984) *What is Politics?* Oxford: Blackwell.

Lemert, E. (1972) *Human Deviance, Social Problems and Social Control*. Boston, London, Melbourne and Henley: Routledge.

Levitas, R. (1985) 'New Right Utopias', *Radical Philosophy*, 39: 3–9.

Lewis, J. (ed.) (1982) *Women's Rights: Women's Welfare*. London: Croom Helm.

Lloyd, C. (1984) *The Man of Reason. 'Male' and 'Female' in Western Philosophy*. London: Methuen.

Lovejoy, A. (1948) *Essays in the History of Ideas*. Baltimore and London: Johns Hopkins University Press.

Lovejoy, A. (1960) *The Great Chain of Being. A Study of the History of an Idea*. New York: Harper & Row.

Lovenduski, J. (1981a) 'Toward the Emasculation of Political Science', pp. 83–97 in D. Spender (ed.), *Men's Studies Modified*. Oxford: Pergamon.

Lovenduski, J. (1981b) *Women in British Political Studies*. Glasgow, Centre for Study of Political Studies: Political Studies Association.

Lukes, S. (1974) *Power: A Radical View*. London: Macmillan.

McAllister, P. (ed.) (1982) *Reweaving the Web of Life*. Philadelphia: New Society Publishers.

McShane, H. and J. Smith (1978) *Harry McShane: No Mean Fighter*. London: Pluto.

Marks, E. (ed.) (1981) *New French Feminism*. Brighton: Harvester.

Marshall, K. (1985) *Moral Panics and Victorian Values*. London: Junius.

Meehan, E. (1985) *Women's Rights at Work: Campaigns and Policy in Britain and the United States*. London: Macmillan.

Meyer, A.G. (1977) 'Marxism and the Women's Movement', pp. 85–112 in D. Atkinson, A. Dallin and G.W. Lapidus (eds), *Women in Russia*. Stanford, CA: Stanford University Press.

Millet, K. (1972) *Sexual Politics*. London: Abacus (first published 1970).

Mitchell, H. (1977) *The Hard Way Up*. London: Virago.

Mitchell, J. (1976) 'Women and Equality', pp. 379–99 in A. Oakley and J. Mitchell (eds) *The Rights and Wrongs of Women*. Harmondsworth: Penguin.

Morgan, D. (1975) *Suffragists and Liberals. The Politics of Woman Suffrage in England*. Oxford: Blackwell.

Mount, F. (1982) *The Subversive Family*. London: Jonathan Cape.

Nozick, R. (1974) *Anarchy, State and Utopia*. Oxford: Blackwell.

Oakley, A. (1982) *Subject Women*. London: Fontana.

O'Brien, M. (1981) *The Politics of Reproduction*. London: Routledge.

O'Brien, P. (1982) *The New Leviathan: The Chicago School and the Chilean Regime 1973–80*. Glasgow: University of Glasgow Institute of Latin American Studies. Occasional Paper 38.

O'Brien, P. (n.d.) 'Old Wine for New Bottles: The Monetarist Experiment in Chile and Britain'. Unpublished mimeo. University of Glasgow.

Okin, S. (1980) *Women in Western Political Thought*. London: Virago (first published 1979).

Okin, S. (1982) 'Women and the Making of the Sentimental Family', *Philosophy and Public Affairs*, 11(1): 65–88.

Pateman, C. (1980) 'The Disorder of Women: Women, Love and the Sense of Justice', *Ethics*, 91: 20–34.

Pateman, C. (1983) 'Feminist Critiques of the Public/Private Dichotomy', pp. 281–303 in S. Benn and S. Gaus (eds), *Public and Private in Social Life*. London: Croom Helm.

Pinchbeck, I. (1930/1969) *Women Workers and the Industrial Revolution, 1750–1850*. New York: Augustus Kelly.

Pizan, C. de (1983 edition) *The Book of the City of Ladies*, E. Richards (trans.), with commentary by M. Warner. London: Picador.

Pollack Petchesky, R. (1981) 'Antiabortion, Antifeminism, and the Rise of the New Right', *Feminist Studies*, 7(2): 206–46.

Prates, S. (1981) 'Women's Labour and Family Survival Strategies under "The Stabilisation Models" in Latin America'. Unpublished mimeo: IDS, University of Sussex.

Radcliffe Richards, J. (1980) *The Sceptical Feminist*. London, Boston, Melbourne and Henley: Rouutledge.

Randall, V. (1982) *Women and Politics*. London: Macmillan.

Randall, V. (1983) 'Teaching about Women and Politics', *Politics*, 3(1): 38–43.

Rawls, J. (1972) *A Theory of Justice*. Oxford: Clarendon Press.

Reich, W. (1970) *The Mass Psychology of Fascism*. London: Souvenir Press (first published 1946).

Reiter, R. (1975) *Toward an Anthropology of Women*. New York: Monthly Review Press.

Riddell, P. (1983) *The Thatcher Government*. Oxford: Martin Robertson.

Rodger, J. (1985) 'On the Degeneration of the Public Sphere', *Political Studies*, XXXII(2): 203–17.

Rover, C. (1967) *Women's Suffrage and Party Politics in Britain 1866–1914*. London: Routledge.

Ruth, S. (1983) 'A Feminist Analysis of the New Right', *Women's Studies International Forum*, 6(4): 345–51.

Sachs, A. and J. Hoff Wilson (1978) *Sexism and the Law*. London: Martin Robertson.

Sanday, P. (1982) *Female Power and Male Dominance*. Cambridge: Cambridge University Press.

Sargent, L. (ed.) (1981) *Women and Revolution: A Discussion of the Unhappy Marriage of Marxism and Feminism*. London: Pluto.

Sayers, J. (1982) *Biological Politics*. London: Tavistock.

Schattschneider, E. (1960) *The Semi-Sovereign People*. New York: Rinehart & Winston.

Schlafly, P. (1977) *The Power of the Positive Woman*. New York: Arlington House.

Schwartz, J. (1984a) 'Participation and Multi-subjective Understanding: an Approach to the Study of Political Participation', *The Journal of Politics*, 46(4): 117–41.

Schwartz, J. (1984b) *The Sexual Politics of Jean-Jacques Rousseau*. Chicago: University of Chicago Press.

Segal, L. (1983) 'The Heat of the Kitchen', pp. 207–15 in S. Hall and M. Jacques (eds), *The Politics of Thatcherism*. London: Lawrence & Wishart.

Siltanen, J. and M. Stanworth (eds) (1984) *Women and the Public Sphere.* London: Hutchinson.

Skinner, Q. (1979) *Foundations of Modern Political Thought.* Vol. I. *The Renaissance.* Cambridge: Cambridge University Press.

Spender, D. (1980) *Man Made Language.* London: Routledge.

Spender, D. (1983) *Women of Ideas and What Men Have Done to Them.* London: Routledge.

Spender, D. (1985) *For the Record.* London: The Women's Press.

Spender, D. (ed.) (1983) *Feminist Theorists.* London: The Women's Press.

Stacey, M. and M. Price (1981) *Women, Power and Politics.* London: Tavistock.

Stanley, L. and S. Wise (1983) *Breaking Out: Feminist Consciousness and Feminist Research.* London: Routledge.

Steinberg, H.J. (1976) '"Workers" Libraries in Germany before 1914', *History Workshop*, 1: 166–80.

Stone, L. (1977) *The Family, Sex and Marriage in England 1500–1800.* New York and London: Harper & Row.

Strong, T. (1982) 'Oedipus as Hero: Family and Family Metaphors in Nietzsche', pp. 173–96 in J. Elshtain (ed.), *The Family in Political Thought.* Brighton: Harvester.

Taylor, B. (1983) *Eve and the New Jerusalem. Socialism and Feminism in the Nineteenth Century.* London: Virago.

Taylor, P., P. Walton and J. Young (1973) *The New Criminology.* London and Boston: Routledge.

Taylor-Gooby, P. (1985) *Public Opinion, Ideology and State Welfare.* London: Routledge.

Thatcher, M. (1979) *Let Our Children Grow Tall.* London: Conservative Political Centre.

Thompson, E.P. (1961) *William Morris: Romantic to Revolutionary.* London: Merlin.

Tomalin, C. (1977) *The Life and Death of Mary Wollstonecraft.* Harmondsworth: Penguin.

Tomlinson, J. (1984) 'Incomes Policies and Women's Wages', *M/F*, 9.

Toynbee, P. (1985) 'The Catholic Whip which Cracks the Rest of Us into Line', *The Guardian*, 17.6.85.

Tracey, M. and D. Morrison (1979) *Whitehouse.* London: Macmillan.

Trumbach, R. (1978) *The Rise of the Egalitarian Family.* New York and London: Academic Press.

Tsukuchi, C. (1961) *H.M. Hyndman and British Socialism.* Oxford: Oxford University Press.

Vallance, E. (1979) *Women in the House.* London: Athlone Press.

Vallance, E. (1982) 'Writing Women Back In', *Political Studies*, XXX(4): 582–90.

Vogel, L. (1983) *Marxism and the Oppression of Women.* London: Pluto.

Wade, N. and W. Broad (1982) *Betrayers of the Truth.* New York: Simon & Schuster.

Walby, S. (1983) 'Women's Unemployment, Patriarchy and Capitalism', *Socialist Economic Review*, 99–114.

Welleck, R. (1981) *A History of Modern Criticism 1750–1950.* Vol 2. *The Romantic Age.* Cambridge: Cambridge University Press.

West London Socialist Society (1983) *The Mass Psychology of Thatcherism*. London: Socialist Society.

Wittgenstein, L. (1979) *The Central Texts of Ludwig Wittgenstein*, G. Brand (ed.). Oxford: Blackwell.

Wolin, S. (1961) *Politics and Vision*. London: Allen & Unwin.

Wollstonecraft, M. (1975) *Vindication of the Rights of Woman*. Harmondsworth: Penguin (first published 1792).

Women's Studies International Forum (1983) *Gatekeeping: The Denial, Dismissal and Distortion of Women*. Special issue 6(5).

Wood, G. (ed.) (1985) *Labelling in Development Policy*. London and Beverly Hills: Sage.

Yates, G. (1977) *What Women Want*. Cambridge, MA, and London: Harvard University Press.

Young, I. (1980) 'Socialist Feminism and the Limits of Dual Systems Theory', *Socialist Review*, 50–51, X(2/3): 169–88.

Index

Notes on contributors

Judith Evans was educated at Manchester, London (London School of Economics) and Essex Universities. Since 1972 she has been a lecturer in Government and Political Studies at Queen Mary College, London. She was a founder member of the Women's Group of the PSA. She is author of various articles on women and politics and is currently writing a book on women and power.

Jill Hills is a lecturer in Communications Policy at City University, and was previously an ESRC Fellow at Manchester University. She is the author of articles on women's political participation and articles and a book on government and industry. She edited *The Politics of the Second Electorate. Women and Public Participation* with Joni Lovenduski (Routledge & Kegan Paul, 1981). She is a long-standing member of the Labour Party and is convenor of the Women's Group of the PSA.

Karen Hunt is a Women's Education Officer for Manchester Local Education Authority and teaches women's studies in adult and higher education. Her research for her PhD is on 'The Woman Question and the Social Democratic Federation, 1880–1914'. She has published in this area and on women and politics.

Elizabeth Meehan is a lecturer in Politics at Bath University. She did her first degree in Politics at Sussex University and a DPhil at Oxford. She is a member of the Executive Committee of the PSA and a previous convenor of the Women's Group. She has been involved in developing a series of seminars on women at Oxford and Bath. Her publications include *Women's Rights at Work: Campaigns and Policies in Britain and the United States* (Macmillan, 1985). Her current research is into social policy (including women's equality) and citizenship in the EEC.

Tessa ten Tusscher has been active in women's politics for ten years. She was educated at Sheffield and York Universities and is currently writing her PhD at Leeds University. During 1985–6 she is Senior Scholar at the University of California, Berkeley, where she is researching the Moral Right in the United States and Britain. She has been a contributor to *Spare Rib* and *Outwrite* for several years.

Ursula Vogel is a lecturer in Government at the University of Manchester. She is editor of the PSA Journal, *Politics*, and a member of the Executive of the PSA.

Georgina Waylen is currently employed as research assistant at Huddersfield Polytechnic, carrying out work on British colonial economic policy in Jamaica in the 1920s and 1930s. The chapter in this volume came out of previous research which she did at Manchester University on the effects of monetarism on women in Chile.